FOR THE LOVE OF THE COUNTRY

UNTOLD STORY OF THE BATTLE OF PELELIU:

A MEMOIR OF JAPANESE COLONEL KUNIO NAKAGAWA

RYUHO OKAWA
IRH Press

Copyright©2015 by Ryuho Okawa
English translation©Happy Science 2015
Original title: "Palau-Shoto Peleliu-to Shubitaicho
Nakagawa Kunio Taisa No Reigen"
All rights reserved
Happy Science is an imprint of IRH Press Co., Ltd.
IRH PRESS
New York . Tokyo
Library of Congress Cataloging-in-Publication Data
ISBN 13: 978-1-941779-62-0
ISBN 10: 194177962X
Printed in the United States of America
Cover Image: ©svenja_9987-Fotolia.com
Interior Image: ©Cabinet Public Relations Office, Cabinet Secretariat
©The National WWII Museum/©Jiji
©CNES 2014/Distribution Airbus DS/IHS

Contents

Publisher's Note 8
Preface 11

○ Opening Comments ○

1. Summoning the Spirit of Colonel Nakagawa, Great Military Commander Who Devastated the Most Powerful Marine Division in the U.S. Military

Taking a fresh look at the Battle of Peleliu, 70 years after the war... 16

A little piece of paradise in the Pacific Ocean that turned into the stage of a deadly struggle between Japan and the U.S., 70 years ago 18

Peleliu, an island now being spotlighted by documentaries and television dramas 20

Reconfirming what exactly happened on the battlefield where the strongest military units of Japan and the U.S. clashed 23

Japanese forces dug caverns out of the coral reef in anticipation of a long, drawn out battle 29

The end of Colonel Nakagawa, after his final telegraph 31

The tough fighting style of the Japanese forces who prevented the U.S. forces from landing troops onto mainland Japan 32

Through this spiritual message, I want to explore the theme, "What is war?" 34

Summoning the spirit of Colonel Nakagawa in precedence to the emperor's visit to Peleliu 37

Spiritual Interview

2. The Truth of the Battle of Peleliu, Revealed by Colonel Nakagawa

"Very, very grateful" for the emperor's visit 39

"I want to answer as faithfully as possible regarding the job we did" 42

"We fulfilled the true mission of a warrior in the Battle of Peleliu" 45

"I don't believe I, or any of my men, died a meaningless death" 47

The reality of the cruel battlefield that Colonel Nakagawa saw with his own eyes 48

The Battle of Peleliu was a defensive war for the mandated territory of Palau 50

The true intention behind the episode in which the islanders were evacuated 52

3. The Meaning Behind the War of Endurance by the Japanese Military

Why did the Japanese forces alter their fighting style so drastically in the Battle of Peleliu? 54

Why the U.S. military and MacArthur were afraid of Japan 56

"People fight for love, they cannot fight out of hatred" 58

The Japanese forces had better tactical and technical battle capabilities 60

The time for the U.S. to reflect on its WWII deeds will come 61

4. Was the Greater East Asia War a War of Invasion or a War to Liberate Colonies?

Japan was a target of U.S. invasion within the trend of invasion by the Western superpowers 67

"There was no aggression on Japan's part in protecting Manchukuo" 72

If Japan didn't fight, the West would've begun to take over China ... 74

Now, 70 years after the war, is the time to reassess history from the Manchurian Incident onward 76

The people of Palau are grateful to Japan for being able to prosper ... 80

China and the USSR became communist countries as a result of the U.S. joining the war 83

5. Colonel Nakagawa Refutes the Lies of Nanking Massacre and Military Comfort Women

The Nanking Massacre is unthinkable considering the Japanese military DNA 86

"Please report the full names of the people who died in Nanking" ... 88

The issue of military comfort women is absolutely ridiculous! 91

China and South Korea's frustration over not winning independence 93

6. Colonel Nakagawa's Way to Protect the Current Japan from China

Japan must become a deterrent to keep China in check 97

Japan's basic goal was "Coexistence and co-prosperity" 101

If the Japan-U.S. alliance is cut off, Okinawa will become a Chinese territory 102

China's national policy of trying to deceive Japan 104

Energy development vital for Japan 106

7. My Wish is for Our People to Regain Their Japanese Pride

"The Japanese people who fought and died have been praying for the prosperity of Japan" 108

Most of the Japanese soldiers who died on Peleliu Island have returned to Heaven 109

Japanese soldiers will be treated as heroes........ 112

The Emperor's visit to Peleliu Island is a blessing 114

Asking about Colonel Kunio Nakagawa's last moments and his post-death experiences 116

"Thinking that we didn't die in vain is the best memorial service for us" 119

8. Where is Colonel Nakagawa Right Now?

Colonel Nakagawa is in a world of war gods with spirits like Masashige Kusunoki........ 121

In his past lives, he fought and fell to protect something great 123

"I feel it's my responsibility to save as many troops as I can, down to the very last man"........ 125

9. Break Free from Materialism and Revolutionize the Times

The bottom line is, "There's more to life than the one on earth" 127

Japan must work to get a higher level of authority and respect 129

"There will be a revolution of the times" 131

Closing Comments

10. Praying that the Spiritual Messages from Colonel Nakagawa Will Influence Public Opinion 134

Afterword 137

About the Author 138

What is a Spiritual Message? 142

About Happy Science 144

Contact Information 146

About the Happiness Realization Party 149

Happy Science University 150

Other Activities 152

About IRH Press 154

Other Books by Ryuho Okawa 155

Spiritual Interview Series 157

IRH Movies 159

Publisher's Note

First and foremost, thank you very much for taking your time and money to read this book. We are grateful for your curiosity and passion to seek the truth. Now, please allow us to explain why we decided to publish *For the Love of the Country —Untold Story of the Battle of Peleliu: a Memoir of Japanese Colonel Kunio Nakagawa*.

The Pacific, an American TV drama series that aired in 2010, featured the fierce battles between the U.S. Marine Corps and the Japanese forces. The drama consisted of 10 total episodes, of which Episodes 5, 6 and 7—the highlights of the series—covered the Battle of Peleliu. The U.S. forces predicted that they would capture the small island in no time; however, the battle lasted over 70 days. This shows how significant the battle was in the entire Pacific War, officially known as Greater East Asia War in Japan.

The drama series was based mainly on the memoirs of two Marines who survived the war and thus emphasized how powerful the Japanese forces were. Where did their power come from? What kind of spirit and goal did they have? Is it true that the Japanese forces were brainwashed by and fought frantically for their fascist government or military, just as the postwar international communities have been saying?

The book you are now reading answers these questions. In these pages, the spirit of Colonel Kunio Nakagawa, garrison commander of Peleliu Island, tells us the untold story of the historical battle between the U.S. Marine Corps and the Japanese forces via *spiritual messages*[*] conducted by Master Ryuho Okawa of Happy Science. This approach is one method of "religious journalism."

"For the Love of the Country" is a phrase taken from the spiritual messages of Colonel Nakagawa. His deep and sublime love was surely not inferior to that of the U.S. soldiers.

This year, 2015, makes 70 years since the end of WWII. Now is the time to ask ourselves, "Is it correct to interpret the Pacific War as a war that fascist Japan lost to democratic America?" What was the true reason for Japan going into WWII? What was Japan trying to accomplish? What kind of influence did Japan have on world history by fighting in the war? There are survivors of WWII out there in the world, even today. We need to gain a true understanding of history and spread it while they are alive.

Americans have the spirit of fair play. They praise their enemies who fought valiantly in battle. Fleet Admiral Nimitz regarded Japanese soldiers who gave

---
[*] For more on spiritual messages, see "What is a Spiritual Message?" near the end of this book.

their lives, "courageous and patriotic" as written on the epitaph on Peleliu.* It is our honest wish that Americans, as well as readers all around the world, further cultivate their spirit of fair play through this book. Not only will this help Japan restore its honor, but also help bring world peace and justice to fight off the growing chaos in this current age.

We would like you to read this book carefully, page by page, word by word, and listen to your inner voice. The colonel's strong sense of love will definitely touch your heart.

For a documentary on Peleliu now and an excerpt of the spiritual message, visit:
https://youtu.be/YTPJIexcmgo

---

*See Chapter 7.

Preface

This year, 2015, marks 70 years since the end of WWII. I expect, in light of that fact, we will see many different views, for and against, being argued. The emperor of Japan, himself, is planning to make a commemorative visit to Palau this April, so there will most likely be all sorts of coverage on the Battle of Peleliu Island in the media as well.

If the most intense decisive battle between Japan and the U.S. on Peleliu Island had been covered accurately and impartially by the U.S. media during WWII, the U.S., which was having difficulty collecting war funds, would most likely have gotten tired of war, right away. And there is a high possibility that some kind of effort would've been put forth to bring an end to the fighting. Of course, there are no "ifs" in history. But "if" that had happened, we can speculate that the Korean War, the Vietnam War and even the Iraq War may not have happened. The Cold War between the U.S. and the Soviet Union could've been avoided. And the enormous, "military first" communist nation that came into being through Mao Zedong's revolution may never have been formed.

The fighting that took place on Peleliu Island was, without a doubt, a defensive battle for Japan. I also want Japanese people everywhere to know that this era also saw a great military commander like the illustrious Masashige Kusunoki*.

> *Ryuho Okawa*
> *Master and CEO of Happy Science Group*
> *March 3, 2015*

---

* Masashige Kusunoki [1290's-1336]: a Japanese military commander and samurai. Kusunoki is popular and respected for his exceptional military strategic skills and loyalty to Emperor Go-Daigo. He received the highest decoration from the Meiji government in 1880.

Kunio Nakagawa (1898–1944)

Military officer. Rose to the position of Lieutenant General in the Imperial Japanese Army [by a two-rank posthumous promotion]. Originally from Kumamoto Prefecture. Graduated from the Imperial Japanese Army Academy and was commissioned as a second lieutenant in the infantry. After ascending to the position of infantry regiment battalion commander, Nakagawa studied at the Army Staff College and earned an army colonel position. He was appointed as regiment commander of the Imperial Japanese Army 2nd Infantry Regiment. The 14th Division, which was affiliated with the 2nd Infantry Regiment, was stationed in the Palau island chain, where Nakagawa was appointed garrison commander for Peleliu Island. He fortified the entire island into a stronghold and led a fierce resistance to cut off the fighting force of the U.S. military, which had planned to take the island. The battle, which lasted for two and a half months, delivered a crippling blow to the U.S. military.

Interviewers:*

Eiichi Satomura
Senior Managing Director of Happy Science
Public Relations and Marketing

Jiro Ayaori
Advanced Executive Director of Happy Science
Chief Editor of *The Liberty*

Yuki Oikawa
Director of Foreign Affairs
Happiness Realization Party

The opinions of the spirits do not necessarily reflect those of Happy Science Group.

---

* Interviewers are listed in the order that they appear in the transcript. Their professional titles represent their positions at the time of the interview.

1

Summoning the Spirit of Colonel Nakagawa, Great Military Commander Who Devastated the Most Powerful Marine Division in the U.S. Military

Taking a fresh look at the Battle of Peleliu,
70 years after the war

RYUHO OKAWA:
This year [2015] is the 70th anniversary of the end of WWII, so I imagine that many news items and articles will be written about the war. We will probably see more television coverage, too.

As for Happy Science, we have been releasing various spiritual messages regarding this matter. Some of these have had quite a major impact, for example, spiritual messages from Hideki Tojo and spiritual messages from Iris Chang [see *The Truth of the Pacific War: Soulful Messages from Hideki Tojo, Japan's Wartime Leader* (New York: IRH Press, 2014), *"Shusho Kotei no Yurei" no Shotai: Tojo Hideki, Konoe Fumimaro, Hirota Koki Nihon wo Shikaru!* (The Truth Behind "Ghosts of the Prime Minister's Residence": Hideki Tojo, Fumimaro Konoe and Koki Hirota Scold Japan!) (Tokyo: IRH

Press, 2013) and *The Secret Behind* The Rape of Nanking: *A Spiritual Confession by Iris Chang* (New York: IRH Press, 2014), all by Ryuho Okawa (see Figure 1)].

Today, I would like to cover Peleliu Island in the Palau island chain. Since the emperor of Japan is planning to make a commemorative visit to the Republic of Palau from the 8th to the 9th of April this year, I believe this topic will be the subject of a lot of attention.

However, there are probably more Japanese people who don't know about Peleliu Island than those who do. For example, even Susumu Nishibe* wrote, about

Figure 1.

Ryuho Okawa, *The Truth of the Pacific War : Soulful Messages from Hideki Tojo, Japan's Wartime Leader* (New York: IRH Press, 2014).

Ryuho Okawa, *The Secret Behind* The Rape of Nanking (New York: IRH Press, 2014).

---

*Susumu Nishibe [1939-present]: a Japanese critic and thinker. Advisor to journal *Hyogensha* [Espressivo] and former professor in the Department of Humanities and Social Sciences at the University of Tokyo.

10 years ago, "I lived to 66 years of age without ever knowing about Peleliu Island." According to this, when he was invited to participate in a group to pay respects at a Peleliu Island gravesite, he said, "What's that? Please bring me some information on it." He read about four books on the topic and learned about the island for the first time in his life.

So, this is how little known the island is. And the reason for that probably has something to do with the U.S. manipulating information on the island.

A little piece of paradise in the Pacific Ocean that Turned into the stage of a deadly struggle between Japan and the U.S., 70 years ago

OKAWA:
On the map, Peleliu Island in Palau is located southeast of the Philippines. It's a very small island, spanning only up to a couple dozen kilometers or so in circumference. During the war, when MacArthur was forced out of the Philippines by Japanese forces, he retreated to Australia with the words, "I shall return." Peleliu Island is close to Leyte Island, which was the island that MacArthur attempted to take once more in the subsequent operation to recover the Philippines.

The large airfield on Peleliu Island [see Figure 2]

• OPENING COMMENTS •

that was known to be the biggest in Asia at the time was built by Japanese forces. It was large enough to house several hundred fighter planes. Because of this, even if MacArthur were able to retake the Philippines, he would suffer serious damage if his forces were bombed from this base. This is why even Admiral Nimitz thought, "Before we land on the Philippines, this simply has to go first. We need to take this base out before we hit Leyte Island."

This is how an island that was often called a little piece of paradise in the Pacific Ocean turned into the stage of a deadly struggle between Japan and the United States.

Figure 2.

Peleliu Airfield: an airfield constructed by Japanese forces during WWII. Occupied by the U.S. Navy during the Battle of Peleliu Island in 1944. Runways stretch out in a cross shape, from north to south and from east to west. Still in use today.

Peleliu, an island now being spotlighted by Documentaries and television dramas

OKAWA:

There are several islands in Palau, in addition to its main island. Peleliu is a small island off the main island [see Figure 3]. With the surrounding area made up mostly of coral reef, Peleliu is an island that resembles a lump of concrete. There isn't a single river there; only one water spring. Japanese forces defended with their very lives, but the U.S. forces eventually reclaimed the spring, bringing an end to their water supply.

The attack was carried out by the 1st Marine Division of the United States Marine Corps. This division had previously captured Guadalcanal Island. It had the reputation of being the bravest division in the U.S. Navy. With high morale from toppling Guadalcanal, they attempted to charge the island all in one swoop.

During all of this, the marines brought with them a camera team of 18 people to capture scenes of U.S. Marine action. Last year, NHK [*Nippon Housou Kyokai*, Japan Broadcasting Corporation] aired a documentary [*The Peleliu Island: A Cruel Battlefield Revisited*, broadcast in English on October 11, 2014 (see Figure 4)] revealing footage of this that has been stored at the U.S. National Archives and Records Administration and underground base storage. In this program, NHK

• OPENING COMMENTS •

Figure 3.

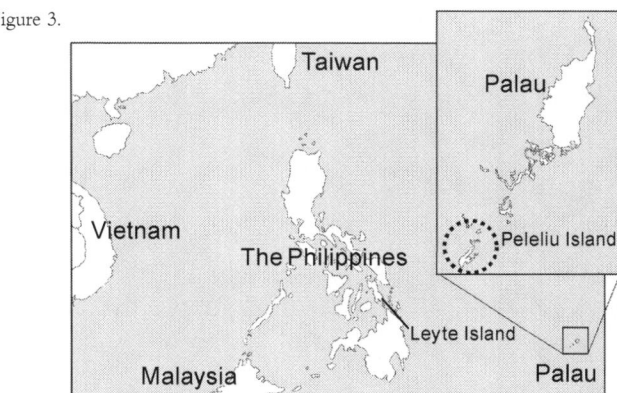

Peleliu Island: an island located in the southwestern part of the Palau island chain. Remnants of warfare, such as tanks and helmets, still spot the island terrain even today, but the vegetation that was incinerated by napalm has grown back, making the island a beautiful sightseeing spot.

Figure 4.

"The Peleliu Island - A Cruel Battlefield Revisited" [NHK special program broadcasted on August 13, 2014] : this documentary featured interviews with the lone survivor out of 18 U.S. cameramen who went to the frontlines and interviews with Japanese soldiers who came back alive.

linked together rare scenes that had been previously hidden. The program included interviews with survivors to report just how cruel this battlefield was and how horrible this war was.

Also, on August 15 of last year, which is the memorial day for the end of the war, Fuji TV aired a story about Peleliu Island garrison commander Kunio Nakagawa [Fuji TV Drama Special Commemorating the End of WWII: *Inochi Arukagiri Tatakae, Soshite Ikinukunda* (As Long as You Still Breathe, Keep Fighting and Stay Alive)] as a prelude to the upcoming 70th anniversary of the end of WWII. I remember a commentary by Akira Ikegami was included both before and after the program.

I thought it was very good that Nakagawa was depicted as an extremely upstanding military commander. And the story also featured a young geisha, on the main island of Palau, who dressed up as a soldier and joined the battle. The show covered how she was called, "Joan of Arc of Peleliu."

• OPENING COMMENTS •

Reconfirming what exactly happened on the Battlefield where the strongest military units of Japan and the U.S. clashed

OKAWA:

Why does Peleliu Island receive so much attention?

As I said earlier, the 1st Marine Division of the U.S. Marine Corps was the division that conquered Guadalcanal and was known as the strongest division in the U.S. Navy. And on the Japanese side, the troops were made up of a regrouping of the Mito and Takasaki regiments of the 14th division of the Kwantung Army* [the command center was in Utsunomiya†], which had been stationed in an area in mainland China that got as cold as 20 degrees below zero [Celsius]. So, this was known as the strongest division on the Japanese side. Thus, in an odd twist of fate, this small island became the stage for a thunderous clash between the most powerful military units in Japan and the U.S., featuring the strongest marine division in the U.S. Navy and the strongest army division in the Japanese military.

---

* Kwantung Army: one of the army groups of the Imperial Japanese Army. This group oversaw the troops stationed in Kwantung [Manchuria].

† Mito, Takasaki, Utsunomiya: cities in the northern part of Kanto region of Japan.

The result was a battle in which the U.S. completely misread Japanese resistance. In fact, the entire thing was also known as "Roosevelt's failure" and was kept secret until the war was over. The U.S. forces, having carved a path of military success all the way up to Guadalcanal Island, seemed to assume, "Looking at the battles fought up to this point, it's best to assume that Japanese forces generally use a waterside strategy where they'll most likely mount attacks at the coastline, in order to halt the enemy from proceeding up onto the land. And in the end, they'll probably make a suicidal attack on us with the *banzai charge**."

Also, in contrast to the American military unit made up of 48,000 soldiers in total, the military unit under the garrison commander Colonel Nakagawa only had about 11,000 soldiers. Because of this, people involved on the U.S. side, including the division commander [Major General William Rupertus], all assumed that the island would fall in about two to three days. There was an optimistic mood like that among the U.S. troops. It's been told that there were even people who thought, "Well, I heard it'll take three days, but I wouldn't be surprised if we finished

---

*Banzai charge: tactical attack by Japanese troops who were out of supplies, out of reinforcements and could not retreat. They considered surrendering and becoming prisoners to be dishonorable. They went charging in toward the enemy, knowing they would be defeated, by yelling, "*Banzai* ['long live'] His Majesty!"

sometime in the morning" or "We might even have a barbeque up on that seashore by this afternoon." That's how sure of themselves they were.

Another reason for that attitude is that airstrikes on the island had already started more than one week before the land invasion was scheduled to take place. In particular, three days before the attack, naval fire from the attack fleet spread out a shell attack of up to several dozen thousands of tons on the small island, turning it into a bald mountain without any trees or shrubbery. Since the onslaught was so heavy, people just assumed there couldn't possibly be anyone alive after that.

So, the shore attack began with the attitude, "After all of this, there shouldn't be many Japanese troops still alive. The U.S. shouldn't lose more than 200 soldiers or so." Yet, they decided to play it cautious, just in case, and dispatched a military unit transport ship which stayed about two kilometers [about 1.2 miles] from the shoreline, where small crafts for landing were unloaded. In other words, they approached the island on special amphibian marine division ships [see Figure 5].

By the way, the Battle of Peleliu Island was depicted in a television miniseries called *The Pacific*, [see Figure 6] which was made by executive producers Steven Spielberg and Tom Hanks and aired in 2010 in the United States. The entire series had ten episodes;

Figure 5.

A U.S. Marine Corps division transferring from an LST [Landing Ship, Tank] to an LVT [Landing Vehicle Tracked] and heading to the coast of Peleliu Island.

Figure 6.

[Left] *The Pacific* [premiered in 2010; executive producers: Steven Spielberg, Tom Hanks and others]

[Right] U.S. forces heading to land in units

• Opening Comments •

the three middle episodes dealt with the Battle of Peleliu Island. The battle became widely known after this television show.

Although the U.S. military arrived with over 40,000 troops, it only sent several thousand marines from the strongest marine division for the first attack wave, since the island was already thoroughly bombed. It's true that Japan suffered heavy losses from artillery bombardment when the U.S. forces landed on the island. However, their assumption that the battle would be over quickly didn't play out as expected.

The Japanese forces decided to put off their traditional style of holding off the enemy waterside and ending with a final banzai charge. Instead, they interconnected the 500 caverns in the coral reef island to transform the entire island into an underground network fortress, with the goal of fighting for as long as possible. Of course, Colonel Nakagawa and all of the troops in his command were prepared to throw away their lives in the fight. However, the strategy was different from previous strategies; he said, "I won't accept any impromptu, unapproved suicide attacks. Drawing the battle out as long as we can will protect our parents, siblings and family and will chip away at America's fighting spirit. We must show them that they can't carve their way up into mainland Japan so easily." So, his order was to draw the battle out as long as possible and to fight until the very end. This battle led up to the subsequent Battle of Iwo-to[*] and Battle of Okinawa. But anyway, we must verify whether or not this battle had any meaning.

In actual fact, the more than 10,000 Japanese garrison was nearly completely wiped out and, in a way, the arena transformed into a fiery Hell. So, there's the question of whether or not this was evil from the viewpoint, "all wars are evil." On the other hand, the U.S. also suffered an equal, or possibly even greater, amount of dead and wounded [Note: Japanese death toll = 10,695. American death toll[†] = 2,336, wounded = 8,450. There were also several thousand American soldiers who incurred mental disorders]. The U.S. side most likely believed they were fighting for God. As for Japan, they worshiped the Japanese gods; for the Japanese, the battle was a fight to protect the nation and the people of Japan.

Where did justice lie in all of this? We can also ask, "Was drawing the battle out and intensifying the damages the right thing to do?" Would it have been better to surrender right away? In this way, I feel that this situation presents us with many points of discus-

---

[*] Iwo-to: an island approx. 1,200 kilometers [approx. 750 miles] away from Tokyo, near the southernmost tip of Ogasawara [Bonin] Islands. Iwo-to was the site of a deadly clash between Japan and the U.S. from February to March of 1945.

[†] Some accounts put damages to U.S. forces at 1,794 dead and 8,010 injured.

sion to think about.

Eleven commendation telegrams were sent from the emperor of Japan, regarding the battle on this island, praising the hard work of the soldiers. Newspapers at the time covered that on their front page.

Japanese forces dug caverns out of the coral reef in Anticipation of a long, drawn out battle

OKAWA:
As I have already said, I believe that the U.S. marines thought they would be able to easily win the battle using fighting methods they had used previously. However, the first marine division to land on the beach, which was a force reported to be around 9,000 or 10,000, took a casualty toll of about 6,500 at the hands of the Japanese military. This is astonishing. When a marine division incurs injury or damage of about 60 percent, this is generally reported as a near-annihilation. So, in other words, the 1st Marine Division of the U.S. Marine Corps, which had a reputation as the strongest force in the Marines, was almost completely destroyed, nearly annihilated.

In this case, however, the injured Marines were put in four medic boats docked in the ocean. The surviving ones were also put on boats. Reinforcements were dispatched after that and they kept trying to successfully stake their claim on beach land. In any case, while the U.S. believed that the battle would be over in two to three days, the Japanese forces wanted a long, drawn out conflict from the very beginning. To this end, they interconnected caverns together, built strong points and resisted the U.S. forces up until the very end.

These caverns were designed in a very complex way so that, even if they received artillery fire from the entrance, the entire force inside wouldn't be demolished. For example, there were caverns where, when you went inside, you would be turned around and led to an exit on the opposite side. But the rock was very hard, so carving it out was very difficult. And though the environment was so harsh that they could only carve out about 20 centimeters [about 8 inches] in a day and though this tiring work continued every single day, they apparently built their stronghold with a pickax.

I've heard that, in the construction of this stronghold, Colonel Nakagawa received much criticism from his comrades in arms. They apparently said things like, "This style of fighting is wrong. This is the fighting strategy of a mole. Burrowing underground and shooting up at enemies on the surface is not the way the Japanese military fights."

• OPENING COMMENTS •

The end of Colonel Nakagawa, After his final telegraph

OKAWA:
So, after the approximately three-day naval bombardment from the U.S. forces ended, the landing operation began on September 15, 1944. The battle lasted until November. The exact number of days for this battle is different depending on which source you consult, with some records saying 71 days, others saying 73 days and yet others saying 74 days. Also, the Fuji TV drama said that the battle lasted 77 days. Whatever the case, sources say that, after a battle of seventy-something days, Colonel Nakagawa sent his last telegraph saying, *"sakura, sakura, sakura"**. He is believed to have taken his own life.

An interpretation opposite to this exists which states, "He was killed by his own military staff because he started to go insane and said that he was going to surrender." However, this information didn't come from someone who was actually on the island. It's a story that someone, who was on a different island, merely heard. It's simply hearsay.

Some believe he committed suicide, others believe

---

* Sakura, sakura, sakura: a Japanese telegram sent to Japan's Palau command headquarters which meant, "Our forces have been defeated." In Japan, the metaphor has traditionally been used to describe a samurai dying in battle by putting up a good fight.

he went insane and died. So, there are all sorts of stories out there. There's no one alive who saw what happened, so there's no way to know for sure. I don't think his body was found, either. But since he was such a prudent individual, he probably took his own life only after running out of ammunition and food rations in the final battle.

There's another story which says, "As the garrison commander, the colonel unsheathed his own sword and went charging in." But we simply don't know the truth.

The tough fighting style of the Japanese forces Who prevented the U.S. forces from landing troops Onto mainland Japan

OKAWA:
In any case, a battle that was expected to be over in two to three days lasted for seventy-something days. Ultimately, MacArthur decided midway to not wait until this island fell before going to Leyte Island; he gave up on waiting and instead had troops land on Leyte before taking Peleliu. Thus, strategically speaking, this battle became meaningless. Despite so, he felt, "If we pull out during mid-battle, the message we imply will be, 'U.S. forces have withdrawn' and that would be used in Japanese military propaganda. We

• OPENING COMMENTS •

can't give up a battle we've already committed to."

Japanese forces went on to adopt this kind of fighting style, fighting for almost 40 days at Iwo-to, too. This is a slightly unrelated story, but concerning the Battle of Iwo-to, there's a famous photograph of 6 U.S. soldiers putting up the Stars and Stripes flag. This photograph decorated the pages of various newspapers [see Figure 7]. The reports made it seem like Iwo-to was occupied in four days, but 3 of those 6 people were killed in subsequent battles. And there's even a story which says that they were killed by their own soldiers.

In fact, the battle continued on for thirty-something days after that, so the U.S. hadn't actually occupied the area yet. What happened was, incorrect reports that the U.S. had won were made. Anyway, the Japanese forces began to put up an extremely tough fight.

Figure 7.

U.S. troops planted their flag on Mount Suribachi during the Battle of Iwo-to [February 23, 1945].

According to one person's story, what happened was, "The U.S. forces began to exhibit fear in the battles at Peleliu Island, Iwo-to and the main island of Okinawa. They knew that having their troops land on mainland Japan would cost the lives of over a million American youths, so they stopped the war in order to prevent that. Japan may have surrendered unconditionally, but the truth is, the Japanese Imperial system was preserved and the surrender was essentially a conditional one due to those battles."

**Through this spiritual message,
I want to explore the theme, "What is war?"**

OKAWA:
The emperor is now 81 years old and is planning to go to Peleliu Island. The island is famously known as the Emperor's Island, so he most likely has a strong sense of duty that's pushing him to make a commemorative visit and collect remains at least once before leaving this world. I suspect this is the way he feels. He has already visited Iwo-to, by the way.

Therefore, I feel that now is the perfect timing to record a spiritual message from Colonel Nakagawa, prior to the emperor's visit. And I would like many people to watch this. Or, this will also be typed out

• Opening Comments •

into book form, so perhaps he might read it.

Also, this spiritual message is our way of commemorating the event.

After Colonel Nakagawa passed away, he was given a two-rank posthumous promotion to the position of lieutenant general. We would like to hear what he has to say about postwar Japan, about the direction that the Abe administration is attempting to head in and about what the Happiness Realization Party is saying. In addition, there's China's path of expansion and all sorts of American wars as well. What does it mean to protect the nation? Should we always avoid war unquestioningly because it's simply too horrid? Did the battlefield that saw over 10,000 people lose their lives transform into a Hell of fire, where everyone is still suffering to this day? Have their souls reached Yasukuni Shrine?* What has become of them?

There are all sorts of issues. So, I want to ask about these sorts of things and explore the theme, "What is war?" Are there things like good and evil, even in war? Is war something that transcends good and evil? These are my concerns.

Furthermore, I understand that Colonel Nakagawa is a great military commander, but I want to know,

---

* Yasukuni Shrine: a Shinto shrine in Chiyoda, Tokyo, Japan. Roughly 2.5 million nation-devoted souls since the end of Edo period are worshiped. The name "Yasukuni," given by Emperor Meiji, represents the nation's wish to preserve peace.

based on the assumption that he and his subordinates were annihilated, if he's taking or if he took some kind of responsibility. Or, perhaps that kind of responsibility didn't arise.

I haven't summoned him yet, so I don't know anything about any of this. Today will be his first appearance.

What's the significance of commemorating souls of the dead at Yasukuni? Moreover, how does he feel about the emperor making such a concerted effort to send him words of praise? I would like to know about these kinds of things, too. The Battle of Peleliu Island is sometimes referred to as "the only failure" of famous American military commander, Admiral Nimitz [see Figure 8]. I wonder if Colonel Nakagawa fought like Yukimura Sanada*.

How exactly should we judge those who persevered in the face of a completely unbeatable attack by over 40,000 troops, without any fighter planes, with tanks that are easily torn apart by artillery fire, without food rations and with weapons becoming increasingly useless? This is what I would like to know. It's a fact that one of America's top marine divisions was wiped out. This must have been very shocking for the U.S., because it hid this fact since the end of WWII. I want to know how that's being judged.

• OPENING COMMENTS •

Summoning the spirit of Colonel Nakagawa
In precedence to the emperor's visit to Peleliu

OKAWA:

Colonel Nakagawa was born in 1898 and is thought to have died at the age of 46, in November 1944.

[*To the interviewers.*] All right, let's get started. Please do well.

[*Puts hands in prayer.*] This is in precedence to the emperor's visit. I summon Colonel Kunio Nakagawa to Happy Science General Headquarters, garrison commander of Peleliu Island in the Palau island chain during WWII, who fought till the end courageously.

I ask you, from the bottom of my heart, to reveal your thoughts and your heart to the people of Japan.

Figure 8.

Fleet Admiral Chester William Nimitz [1885–1966]: fought against Japanese forces during WWII as the U.S. Commander in Chief of Pacific Ocean Areas and as the commander with operational control over the three forces of Allied Powers [air, ground and sea] in the Central Pacific Area.

---

*Yukimura Sanada [1567–1615]: a military commander from the Azuchi-Momoyama period to the early Edo period. Second son of Masayuki Sanada. He was active as a military commander for the Toyotomi forces during the Osaka Campaign, which took place in the early Edo period. His bravery as a military leader is recorded in the historical archives of the Edo shogunate and various daimyo lords. It is said that Sanada daringly challenged Ieyasu Tokugawa.

The spirit of Peleliu Island garrison commander, Colonel Kunio Nakagawa.

Please descend to Happy Science General Headquarters and reveal to us your thoughts and your heart.

The spirit of Peleliu Island garrison commander, Colonel Kunio Nakagawa.

Please descend to Happy Science General Headquarters and reveal to us your heart.

[*About 20 seconds of silence.*]

2

The Truth of the Battle of Peleliu, Revealed by Colonel Nakagawa

"Very, very grateful" for the emperor's visit

KUNIO NAKAGAWA:
[*Exhales slowly.*]

EIICHI SATOMURA:
Please excuse me for asking. Are you Colonel Kunio Nakagawa?

KUNIO NAKAGAWA:
[*Lifts face slowly and nods enthusiastically.*] Hmm… Yes!

SATOMURA:
We are extremely grateful that you've taken the time to descend to Happy Science General Headquarters today, February 24, 2015, 70 years after the end of WWII.

KUNIO NAKAGAWA:
Sure. All of you are doing good work.

Peleliu Island garrison commander Colonel Kunio Nakagawa

As evidenced by his entrance into the Army War College after turning 40, Kunio Nakagawa was an upstanding soldier who followed a solid and self-made career advancement path in a way that was clearly different from the privileged elite class. For a short time, an arms reduction after WWI resulted in the unfortunate transfer to being a commissioned officer attached to a school where he spent several years as an instructor at a junior high school. However, he took a command post on the frontlines during the Second Sino-Japanese War where his capabilities as a commanding officer during actual warfare were recognized.

Right after he arrived to his post at Peleliu Island, he took the initiative to board a bomber aircraft and scout out the coral reef and vegetation on the island. Though he constantly engaged in strategic thinking that focused on actual warfare as opposed to theory, he was also said to be the type of person who paid great attention to minor details and had a quiet, serious side.

SATOMURA:
Thank you. After your death, you were appointed to the position of lieutenant general. However, since we want to speak mainly about your time on Peleliu Island, please allow us to address you as colonel.

KUNIO NAKAGAWA:
That's good enough.

SATOMURA:
Thank you very much.

My first question is, "Are you aware that His Imperial Majesty is planning to visit Peleliu Island this coming April [2015]?" And what are your thoughts on the emperor visiting the island? I would like to begin our discussion by hearing what you have to say regarding these questions.

KUNIO NAKAGAWA:
Yes, I've heard about the planned visit. I'm very grateful. I'm truly, truly grateful that His Imperial Majesty still thinks about us, even after 70 years have passed.

SATOMURA:
OK. And in fact, you received commendations from Emperor Showa[*] praising the defense military unit on

---
[*] Emperor Showa [1901-1989]: the 124th Emperor of Japan. Reigned from 1926 to 1989.

Peleliu Island, as many as 11 times.

KUNIO NAKAGAWA:
Yes. Truly grateful.

SATOMURA:
So, about this...

KUNIO NAKAGAWA:
I'm just very, very grateful.

SATOMURA:
I see.

"I want to answer as faithfully as possible Regarding the job we did"

SATOMURA:
Also, right now, we're heralding the 70th year since the end of the war. Would it be correct to say that you know most of the flow since the war ended?

KUNIO NAKAGAWA:
Yes. I'm informed about most of it.

• SPIRITUAL INTERVIEW •

SATOMURA:
Ah, OK. Thank you. Then, today, we would like to ask you about things that happened during the war and, as this year is the 70th anniversary since the end of WWII, about your thoughts on what went on between that time and now, as well as your thoughts on the present situation.

KUNIO NAKAGAWA:
Well, I don't have enough knowledge or experience to speak on national defense as a whole or the policy of our nation, so I do want to say up front that I can't really offer any opinion from a wide perspective. However, I do want to answer your questions as faithfully as I can regarding things like the job we did, what came with that and what happened as a result.

SATOMURA:
Thank you very much. We've actually already spoken to individuals such as Prime Minister Hideki Tojo and General Iwane Matsui in the form of a spiritual message [see Ryuho Okawa, *The Truth of the Pacific War: Soulful Messages from Hideki Tojo, Japan's Wartime Leader* and *"Shusho Kotei no Yurei" no Shotai: Tojo Hideki, Konoe Fumimaro, Hirota Koki Nihon wo Shikaru!* (The Truth Behind "Ghosts of the Prime Minister's Residence": Hideki Tojo, Fumimaro Konoe and Koki

Hirota Scold Japan!) as already cited, as well as *What Really Happened in Nanking?: A Spiritual Testimony of the Honorable Japanese Commander Iwane Matsui* (New York: IRH Press, 2015)(see Figure 9)].

However, it's an extremely rare opportunity for us to be able to speak to a soldier who, please excuse my crude expression, "worked his way up" by actually fighting in the battlefields. So, we would be very honored if you could share your story with us today, including things like how things really were on the battlefield during the war.

KUNIO NAKAGAWA:
Yes. Certainly. Yes.

Figure 9.
Ryuho Okâwa, *What Really Happened in Nanking?: A Spiritual Testimony of the Honorable Japanese Commander Iwane Matsui* (New York: IRH Press, 2015)

"We fulfilled the true mission of a warrior In the Battle of Peleliu"

SATOMURA:
As Master Ryuho Okawa explained earlier, the Battle of Peleliu, which started on September 15, 1944 and ended in the end of November, featured the annihilation of the 1st Marine Division, which was known as the toughest division in the United States.

Looking back from the standpoint of today, how do you feel about the overall battle?

KUNIO NAKAGAWA:
Well, I think we fulfilled the true mission of a warrior because, you see, it was a fight in which we knew, from the very beginning, that we would be completely demolished. And the telegraph message I sent at the end which said, *"sakura, sakura, sakura"* signified that a cherry blossom will unquestioningly fall. But will you let it fall in a day, three days, a week or a month? Two or three months? The question was, "How long can we make that cherry blossom last?"

It was very difficult for me to commit to this and take this upon myself as my mission, since I knew well that this will make my troops suffer that much longer. Just now you said that the battle ended in seventy-something days, but over 30 people from my garrison actually survived that battle and continued fighting until 1947. There were people who continued fighting even one year and eight months after the war officially ended. So, everyone needs to know that there were people who continued fighting until 1947, holding fast to the order I issued to, which was, "Live on and keep fighting until the very end." They did an amazing job.

SATOMURA:
Only thirty-something, out of a unit of ten thousand Japanese soldiers, survived to the end. And these people continued living inside the caverns, never stopping their unrelenting resistance until April 1947.

KUNIO NAKAGAWA:
In the end, the U.S. troops were too afraid to even set foot in these caverns without setting them ablaze with flamethrowers or pouring fuel and lighting it. So, they did all sorts of things like that. They would take a bulldozer and cover up holes. I believe some soldiers ended up being buried alive. But the entire island was a stronghold of 500 caverns, so it was entirely possible for my troops to find ways to survive somewhere, somehow.

Nevertheless, the battle was intense.

SATOMURA:
Yes.

"I don't believe I, or any of my men, Died a meaningless death"

SATOMURA:
You said that you were fully prepared to fall. At what point, in your transfer from Manchuria to Palau, did you have that determination?

KUNIO NAKAGAWA:
Well, that's a military secret, so I can't divulge that. All I can really say on that subject is, I did feel I was going to a place where all I would need is summer clothing. I can't even speak of the details with my own family, but I did at least know that I was going from a cold place to a warm place. I mean, we went from fighting in a severely cold zone to fighting on a tropical island that could be around 35 to 36 degrees Celsius or even all the way up to 45 to 46 degrees Celsius at times. So, I do think that I made my men experience both "Frigid Hell" and "Hell of Flames" or "Fiery Hell."

The responsibility for the death of more than 10,000 men I had serving under me is definitely mine, of course. But I don't believe I, or any of my men, died a meaningless death.

The U.S. forces were definitely spreading all kinds of prejudiced and disparaging propaganda against Japan, but they quietly hid the fact that they also suffered a humiliating defeat, which, I think, points to the fact that they were probably amazed at how brave and powerful the Japanese forces were. Therefore, what they did was they diverted attention from Peleliu Island by thoroughly publicizing their success in the Invasion of Normandy. The truth is, although what happened during the invasion of Peleliu was worthy of its own movie as well, the entire thing was kept a secret.

Of course, that kind of propaganda battle is an inevitable part of war, so it's understandable why they attempted to use it in that way. In other words, we prevented them from doing what they wanted to do, which was to show in movies how quickly they occupied the area in order to raise war morale. I guess that was their plan.

The reality of the cruel battlefield that Colonel Nakagawa saw with his own eyes

JIRO AYAORI:
NHK recently broadcast the video footage of the Battle of Peleliu in a documentary. The title was, *The Peleliu Island: A Cruel Battlefield Revisited* [NHK special program].

Can you tell us about the actual battlefield as you saw it with your own eyes?

KUNIO NAKAGAWA:

Well, if you say that war was cruel, then yes, it certainly was, if seen by others. It's cruel to people who weren't involved. To people in your era, it must seem like gathering people up inside a wired fence and making them fight to death, over and over again. So, if you want to say that the battle was cruel, then yes, it certainly was. It really was like beasts being locked in a cage and fighting to death. In that sense, the battle certainly was cruel.

But you know, for us, it was cruelty that had calmness and composure. Each one of us was fighting with exact awareness of what was going on. To the Americans, however, it was a battle where some of them went insane. There was a constant stream of, "No way!" "This can't be true!"

The U.S. forces really just came thinking that they could conquer us in two to three days. So, the cruelty had to be overwhelming when the deadly struggle extended to seventy-something days and they saw almost all of their friends and people that they knew die or get injured. It must've been overwhelming when the area just became full of corpses and there were piles of the dead and the wounded. It must've been overwhelming when they saw people getting taken away on medic ships with a missing arm or with no legs.

The Battle of Peleliu was a defensive war
For the mandated territory of Palau

AYAORI:
I apologize for asking such a rude question, but I think what NHK tried to do was to show content that would sort of guide the viewer into feeling, "This battle was totally pointless. It was based on cruelty and had absolutely no meaning." What do you...

KUNIO NAKAGAWA:
Well, yes, I understand that such type of coverage could've existed. The thing is, people need to know, "Japan didn't pillage and occupy Peleliu Island." You see, the Palau island chain was, in fact, a territory that was mandated to Japan by the LN [League of Nations] after being torn apart by Germany in WWI. Japan had built schools, hospitals and roads there. Japan provided direction for agriculture and brought wealth to the nation. Japan also taught the Japanese language to the locals. The islands became bountiful and I hear people there are still grateful for all of that. [See Figure 10.]

SATOMURA:
Yes, that's true.

• SPIRITUAL INTERVIEW •

KUNIO NAKAGAWA:

So, basically, that battle was purely defensive for us. The enemy were the ones invading. We weren't invading anywhere, so we weren't an invading army. The islanders said, "We want to fight together with you." But we responded, "No, we're the war experts here, so we'll be the only ones to die. We don't want a single islander to die." I mean, they did help us dig holes, but as soon as we heard that the enemy fleet was on its way, we evacuated all of the islanders to the main island and entered into battle prepared to die.

Figure 10.

During the period of Japanese control after WWI, various kinds of infrastructure and maintenance proceeded, focusing around Koror Island, the most populated island in the Palau island chain. Since there were a large percentage of Japanese residents at the time, it's not uncommon to hear Japanese-style names for cities and people, even today.
[Right] Koror 3rd Street during the South Pacific Mandate era
[Upper left] Koror post office
[Lower left] Telecommunications tower constructed in Palau

So, you know, for a long time now, everyone has been saying that the Japanese forces were the bad guys here, that we were the invaders. But the proof that we weren't invading at all lies in the things I just said. We were a defensive force. The people living there were thankful to Japan. They continued being thankful to Japan after the war. This is how they felt. But these things weren't reported fairly.

People have to realize this: countries like India and what's now called Sri Lanka were once colonies; they were liberated. What I'm saying is, "Japan didn't do a single thing wrong in all of that. In fact, all of these places owe gratitude to Japan for their current independence." But the world doesn't see this as a valid statement, so I feel it's very important to have people know the truth about Peleliu.

The true intention behind the episode In which the islanders were evacuated

AYAORI:
There's an episode that some people talk of, even now. The story goes like this. "The Palau islanders went up to Colonel Nakagawa saying, 'We want to fight together.' But he supposedly said to them at the end, when he made them evacuate, 'The Japanese army

could never fight together with you *dojin* [Japanese word for "savages" or uncivilized people].' Supposedly, Colonel Nakagawa said this very harsh thing to them right before he made them evacuate. But when the evacuation boat left the shore, Japanese troops started singing the songs that they had once sung together with the islanders and saw them off." This is the way the story goes, but the truth hasn't been verified.

Did this really happen?

KUNIO NAKAGAWA:

Yeah. I think it was close to that. I mean, of course, as a garrison commander, the basic mission is to protect the area and keep it safe. So, I couldn't really say that we were going into battle to die. It wouldn't make sense logically if I said, "We will protect this island" but turned around and told everyone to evacuate. If the Japanese troops were really protecting the people there, then they should be able to stay there and live their lives.

But we knew that the enemy attack wouldn't be of such scale. We already knew that the entire island would become a honeycomb. That's why we built that kind of a cavern stronghold.

I might've spoken a bit harshly, but that was only because I didn't want a single one of the islanders to die. I had to cut off our attachment to them, so I sent them away by force. That's what I did. But I believed that they understood my true intentions.

3

The Meaning Behind the War of Endurance by the Japanese Military

Why did the Japanese forces alter their fighting Style so drastically in the Battle of Peleliu?

SATOMURA:
Earlier, you used the words 'brave' and 'calm' to describe the Japanese forces. I feel that, up until before the Battle of Peleliu, the bravery of Japan had been displayed in the willingness to choose an honorable suicidal fighting. Recently, this is often compared to the suicide bombing of Islamic extremists. But let's set that aside for the moment. The fact remains that you completely changed the Japanese fighting style to a war of endurance, where you dig in and stand your ground until the very last moment.

You dug out caverns in a coral reef island in an extremely calm and rationally calculated manner. So, people like myself who live in the present wonder,

"Why did you change to that kind of a style?" How should we take this?

KUNIO NAKAGAWA:
I see. Well, first off, you have to understand that the Imperial Headquarters was also starting to change the strategy, so it wasn't a unilateral decision on my part. What was happening at that point was, Guadalcanal and various other islands began to fall. And they fell in such rapid succession. We knew that, if these islands were to fall one after the other, the enemy would come attacking into mainland Japan too quickly. So, one policy for dealing with this was to spread dissatisfaction toward war amongst the American people by slowing this down and drawing it out as much as possible, resulting in greater enemy casualties.

If the number of casualties goes up, anti-war movements would pop up within the United States. And since it's a nation that places importance on humanitarianism, if people hear about their family members, acquaintances or friends dying, a mood of dissatisfaction toward war would gradually start to take root. I mean, it's true that we have to open up the path to peace somewhere. But if you don't deliver a certain amount of blows to your enemy, you won't be able to obtain peace.

So, our mindset was basically this. We knew we weren't strong enough to actually win against the enemy, but we tried to engage in the most fierce battle and hit the enemy with a strength nearly equal to its own, on this southern front. We tried to make the battle last as long as possible. While doing that, we tried to deal heavy blows to the enemy, so that there would eventually be some form of mediation. We wanted the war to end without the enemy ever making it into mainland Japan. We wanted to preserve the system of having an emperor reign over Japan.

Why the U.S. military and MacArthur Were afraid of Japan

YUKI OIKAWA:
I think that strategy definitely had some impact on the United States. If it weren't for the Battle of Peleliu, the U.S. would've immediately set sights on Tokyo.

KUNIO NAKAGAWA:
Yeah.

OIKAWA:
So, would it be correct to say that the reason why the U.S. took the battle to Okinawa was that you made them afraid of this kind of fighting?

KUNIO NAKAGAWA:

Well, if [both Japan and the U.S.] suffered the same number of casualties, that means an American died for every Japanese person killed. So, let's say you calculated just how many people you have to kill in order to invade and take control of Japan. If the same amount of people on your side has to die, that would be an immense figure.

The biggest war the U.S. ever had was the Civil War. That war had about 600,000 [deaths]. Wars other than that just didn't... Well, OK, the one in Vietnam [the Vietnam War], which came after our battle on Peleliu, I think the U.S. lost about a little over 50,000 people. So, they haven't had any higher casualty rate than the Civil War. In terms of war, I mean.

So, an expectancy of casualties in the millions is more than enough to give strategy leaders cause for doubts [about invading mainland Japan]. If more than 10,000 U.S. troops were wounded or killed at Peleliu Island, then a simple calculation would reveal this. They knew that Japan had at least a million soldiers, so the thought of all of those one million setting out to achieve an honorable suicide, with the goal of each killing a single U.S. soldier, must've been horrifying.

What's more, I heard that when MacArthur set foot on Atsugi* smoking his pipe, his legs were shaking in fear. He didn't actually think that he could land safely in Japan. The truth is, he was afraid of being done in by a sniper or cut down by a sword. I imagine that the tradition of a samurai nation was indeed frightening.

"People fight for love, They cannot fight out of hatred"

SATOMURA:
In terms of number of soldiers, the Japanese forces only had about one-fourth to one-fifth the size of the enemy. And if you include aviation forces, I believe they only had one-sixth or, actually, one-tenth the power. I'm very puzzled; how did you hold up your own morale in fighting with such a small force? How did you convey that to your men to keep their morale up as well? I'm wondering, "What kept everyone's morale from dropping?" Could you tell us about that?

KUNIO NAKAGAWA:
Hmm. Well, when all is said and done, people simply can't fight out of hatred. The human heart is something that fights for love. You can't kill Americans simply out of hatred.

---

* This is in reference to August 1945, shortly after the end of the Pacific War, when Supreme Commander for the Allied Powers Douglas MacArthur arrived in Atsugi of Kanagawa Prefecture.

So, we fight for things like the love of our country, the love of our family and the need to protect our people. [*Nods slightly, closes mouth firmly and becomes slightly teary.*]

SATOMURA:
Hearing that, I think of how even now, in modern television dramas, especially with the aforementioned NHK, the soldiers or the people going to war are always depicted as if they were insane. The characters say things like, "the Americans and the British are devils" and just attack out of utter hatred. But you're saying that's not how it was...

KUNIO NAKAGAWA:
People can't fight out of hatred. They can't fight out of hatred only. This is how we felt: "Holding out for one more day means delaying the attack on our country one more day. Our own deaths will prevent thousands and tens of thousands of our people back home from dying." So, if possible, we wanted to take the fight to a level that would chip away at the U.S. military's will to fight. We wanted to do whatever we could to make them feel, "This is a futile fight, so we should just stop."

We didn't have any battleships by then. We didn't have any aircraft carriers or fighter planes by then.

The major flow of war seemed to be taking us toward defeat, since our "Absolute National Defense Zone" was being breached. However, delivering as much damage as we could to the other side and chipping away at their will to fight would create the conditions that would allow Japan to close the curtains on this war in an advantageous position. So, we believed, "The loss of 10,000 lives is not in vain."

Japan would've easily been trampled if things went like our enemies had anticipated: if we were occupied in half a day or by noon, raised a white flag of surrender and if they planted their Stars and Stripes atop a rocky mountain, only to enjoy barbeque on the beach for lunch. But I believe we showed them that taking Japan will be no easy feat.

The Japanese forces had better Tactical and technical battle capabilities

KUNIO NAKAGAWA:

They burned out caverns with flamethrowers. The flame must've had a range of somewhere around 130 meters to 150 meters [430 feet to 490 feet, roughly]. Making those things for the purpose of burning other humans to death is nothing more than burning people alive, just like the medieval times.

In other words, they were too frightened to get close to us without doing so first. They were too afraid to approach the cavern holes. That was because we were actually much better in sniping. Of course, we were low on ammunition, so we had to hit and kill the enemy with a single shot. The 14th division of the Kwantung Army was better at that kind of sharpshooting. I mean, yes, we had enough bombardment skill to reach all the way to the enemy forces climbing up the coastline, to hit things like tanks from mountaintops and totally demolish them.

So, I believe we had the upper hand in terms of tactical and technical battle capabilities. But the difference in goods and arms performance, as well as the fact that we didn't have resources, meant that there was just no way we could ever hope to win. If we had the same amount of resources, we probably wouldn't have lost.

The time for the U.S. to reflect on Its WWII deeds will come

AYAORI:
This next question is a bit difficult to ask. Some coverage in the media, including the NHK coverage we mentioned earlier, takes the view, "In the Battle of

Peleliu Island, or the subsequent battle at Iwo-to, Japan displayed a rigid resistance in ground fighting. But this only led to the Great Tokyo Air Raids [see Figure 11] and maybe even to the use of the atomic bomb." What are your thoughts on this?

KUNIO NAKAGAWA:
Well, it's just that the time for the U.S. to reflect on its WWII deeds hasn't fully come yet. So, in other words, I can't speak fully on this because they haven't yet come to the point of feeling remorse for their actions. But I do think that, at some point, the time for that kind of reflection and remorse will come.

I mean, even when they fought us, they did things like set us ablaze with flamethrowers. And they completely bombarded and bombed the entire island until they thought not even a single person remained. Only then did they carefully come ashore, upon which they experienced more than 10,000 casualties before retreating. In other words, their first wave of Marines was smashed to pieces, so they had to fight by asking for reinforcements.

They came up onto Peleliu Island in such state. They came to occupy the airfield, but they ended up taking overwhelming damages and even suffered night raids. Basically, many of them lost it and went mad.

SATOMURA:
Right.

KUNIO NAKAGAWA:
Yeah. I mean, think about it from the viewpoint of the invaders. Burning the insides of caverns with flamethrowers or pouring heavy oil in and setting that ablaze to burn the entire insides of the caverns. [See Figure 12.] Could you stand that as a human being? You'd go crazy, right?

Figure 11.

Great Tokyo Air Raids: since 1944, over 100 bombing raids were carried out on Tokyo by the U.S. military's B-29 bombers. Of these, the affected in air raids on March 10, 1945 in particular exceeded one million people.

Figure 12.

The U.S. military's armored vehicle with flamethrower capability. The U.S. forces, which had already incurred a massive amount of casualties, attempted to turn the tide of a deadly war scenario with these cutting-edge weapons. These weapons could actually blow fire into the caves where Japanese troops hid, from over 100 meters away.

SATOMURA:
Yes.

KUNIO NAKAGAWA:
OK. And they did the same kinds of things at the battles of Iwo-to and Okinawa. So, I think they really must've felt as if they had gone insane. Furthermore, they thought up a lethal weapon that was even more efficient because they didn't want to die. I'm talking about the napalm bombs [see Figure 13] that were used on our island. These produced high temperatures of 1,000°C over the island, creating a flame-filled environment where absolutely no living thing could survive.

What's more, they didn't just use this against Japan. They also used napalm to burn farmers in Vietnam, which came after WWII. I think the U.S. had to deal with a lot of guilt over this. I guess no one is allowed to use napalm bombs anymore, but the point is, the enemy's strategy was to one-sidedly massacre us while staying in a completely safe place. They did things on a scale that gave them no right to criticize Hitler's holocaust. Also, burning 100,000 people alive in one night through the Great Tokyo Air Raids during War Plan Orange[*] was not something that a normal human being could do.

Knowing that Japanese houses were made of wood

and paper, they formed a plan to completely burn down the houses. They studied the most efficient way; they surrounded the area on all four sides and completely burned down the houses. There were mounds of corpses at the end. I'm sure the rivers were filled with floating bodies, too.

Then they dropped "bombs of the devil" on Hiroshima and Nagasaki. The U.S. will, slowly but surely, need to reflect on all of this. Some of our people may think, "We were attacked with such powerful weaponry because we resisted." But, you know, the attackers must've really felt inhumane and cowardly.

Figure 13.

Napalm bombs, which were also used in the Vietnam War. The flames burn at extremely high temperatures and can incinerate a large area of land. These flames are oil-based, so it is very difficult to put them out with regular water once they come into contact with a human body or foliage. The fire blazes on for a long period of time. Due to these features, they were used widely in many different wars. However, napalm bombs were subjected to repeated criticisms saying that using them is excessive cruelty.

---

*War Plan Orange: in the beginning of the 20th century, the U.S. Navy developed a color-coding project which assigned different colors to countries that were considered possible war threats. Among these, "War Plan Orange" was the title for the war plans that considered Japan, which had emerged victorious from the Russo-Japanese War, as a potential enemy. The plan proposed an attack on Japan from the Philippines, which would serve as a frontline base.

So, some people want to make them [the U.S. forces] some kind of heroes, but people who dropped the atomic bomb can't possibly be called heroes. We're not scorpions, you know?

SATOMURA:
Right.

KUNIO NAKAGAWA:
We're not scorpions in the Nevada desert. Anyhow, you know, this country that killed its own brothers and sisters is calling out for humanitarianism now. But the truth is, there's reflection behind this humanitarianism. Reflection on themselves, that is.

• SPIRITUAL INTERVIEW •

4

Was the Greater East Asia War A War of Invasion or A War to Liberate Colonies?

Japan was a target of U.S. invasion
Within the trend of invasion
By the Western superpowers

SATOMURA:
Just now, you talked about how the U.S. did things.

KUNIO NAKAGAWA:
Yeah.

SATOMURA:
Looking at it from that viewpoint, earlier you said, "The Battle of Peleliu Island was a defensive war for the Palau island chain." But what is becoming an issue again now, during the 70th anniversary since the end of WWII, is this: when things developed into the Greater East Asia War, was that war a war of invasion inflicted by Japan? Or, instead, was it a defensive battle and a battle to liberate the colonies in Asia? This is a debate that's still going on to this day.

Looking at this from your viewpoint of actually being on the battlefield at the time, I would like to ask you what your thoughts are regarding the question, "Was the Greater East Asia War really a war of invasion instigated by Japan?"

KUNIO NAKAGAWA:
I think the Japanese people tend to focus their thoughts on Japan too much. If you look at this from the perspective of world history, you can see that the Western superpowers have been invading for a very long time. Hundreds of years. What Japan did was only for dozens of years. Therefore, "What Japan did was the only bad thing. Everything before it was not bad" just doesn't make any sense.

The Palau island chain was previously ruled by German forces. India was under British rule for 150 years, but it didn't get any better as a nation.

SATOMURA:
Right.

KUNIO NAKAGAWA:
It stayed poor. It was exploited. It was the perfect example of what it's like to be exploited. To tell the truth, *Capital* by Marx is based on that kind of colonial exploitation.

• SPIRITUAL INTERVIEW •

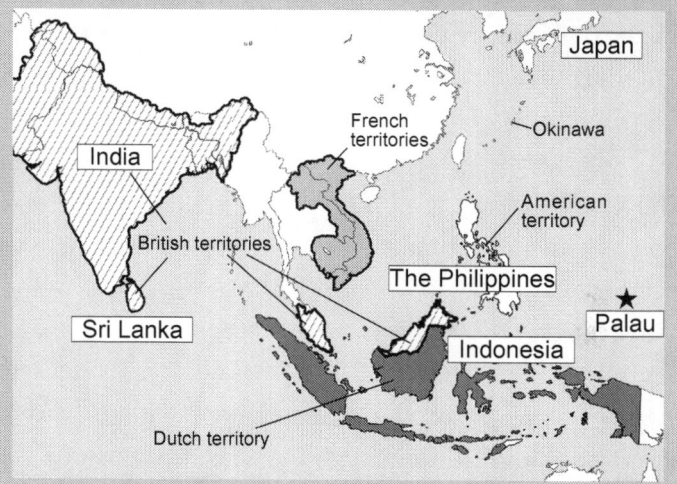

Asia under Western rule [as of 1944]

During WWII, various Asian countries were being colonized by Western superpowers like the U.S. and the Netherlands.

The Palau island chain was freed from German colonial rule after WWI and had become a mandate of Japan. Palau then enjoyed development in infrastructure, mainly on Koror Island. But during WWII, Peleliu Island had become a concern to Allied forces since it housed a large airfield which functioned as a key base for naval activity. As a result, Peleliu became the site of a fierce battle between Japan and the United States. The major colonies in South and Southeast Asias that belonged to Western superpowers at that time were as below.

British territories: India, Sri Lanka, Malaysia
French territories: Vietnam, Laos, Cambodia
American territory: The Philippines
Dutch territory: Indonesia

SATOMURA:
Yes.

KUNIO NAKAGAWA:
So, there's that kind of thing, too. And somewhere like Indonesia was ruled by a foreign power.

SATOMURA:
Yes, by the Netherlands.

KUNIO NAKAGAWA:
Yes, that's right. And the U.S. rallied a fighting spirit as the victims of an attack on Hawaii with hatred for Japan and slogans like "remember Pearl Harbor." But if you ask whether Hawaii was a U.S. territory, the answer is that Hawaii was an independent kingdom. The U.S. basically plundered a territory that was under the Kamehameha Dynasty founded by Kamehameha I.

SATOMURA:
Yes.

KUNIO NAKAGAWA:
And after that, the Philippines was also made into a U.S. colony.

SATOMURA:
Yes.

KUNIO NAKAGAWA:
If you spread out a world map and look at it, the Philippines are directly below Japan or, in other words, located to the south of it. They came this far to obtain the area, so we could definitely foresee the Battle of Okinawa. You can see this from the geographical sense.

Thus, there's absolutely no way the U.S. can say it didn't intend to invade. The U.S. couldn't invade India, since it was under British control. So, bearing that in mind, the countries that were available as targets for U.S. invasion were, of course, Japan, South Korea, the Korean Peninsula and China.

SATOMURA:
Yes.

KUNIO NAKAGAWA:
The target which came after the Philippines was, without a doubt, here.

SATOMURA:
Yes.

KUNIO NAKAGAWA:
This is something that the Japanese understood from as early as the Meiji period. We knew that we would eventually clash with the United States. It's fine to look at this as a matter of "good or evil" or "right or wrong." But if you look at in hindsight, the history of the world has been forged in such balance of power. The trend of power politics, in which hegemonic states that had gained power expand their territory, was something that had continued for hundreds of years. Japan came in the very end of that.

"There was no aggression on Japan's part In protecting Manchukuo"

AYAORI:
You were stationed in mainland China for a very long time. And it's generally thought that Japan invaded China. On the other hand, there were all sorts of internal struggles going on in China, from conflict between powers like the Chinese Nationalist Party and the Chinese Communist Party. To add, powers like the U.S., Great Britain and Germany were interfering in that. So, there was a sort of proxy war going on.

From your point of view, what are your thoughts regarding the claim, "Japan invaded China"?

KUNIO NAKAGAWA:
Well, the China that Japan fought was Qing Dynasty China. We fought them in the First Sino-Japanese War and won. They paid us reparations and ceded their land, too.

I'm sure you all must've studied this in your Japanese history courses, but the Triple Intervention was forced upon us by, I believe, Germany, France and Russia. By this Triple Intervention, we were pressured to return the land we won. The sense of humiliation of the people at that time must've been incredible. Germany, France and Russia... It was very difficult to forgive what they did.

SATOMURA:
Yes.

KUNIO NAKAGAWA:
From there, it was obvious that the southerly advancing Russia had their eyes on the Korean Peninsula. Everyone thought that Russia would most likely advance southward. And as for the Qing Dynasty, it ended up getting into all sorts of internal conflicts and were pushed back all the way to Manchuria as a result of losing the First Sino-Japanese War. That's why we established the independent country of Manchukuo.

This was called a "puppet regime" and is spoken

ill of in Japanese history. But the truth is that the Manchu people, not the Han Chinese, were controlling China. So, what you have here is a place that was torn apart by internal warfare. Considering that the Japanese Imperial Household was bound in a marital relationship with Manchukuo, the independence of that state and subsequent backing is the kind of thing that, from a historical point of view, many nations other than Japan would have also done. So, I don't think this can really be called aggressive.

This is why I believe that the protection of Manchukuo by the Japanese army wasn't of an aggressive nature.

If Japan didn't fight, The West would've begun to take over China

KUNIO NAKAGAWA:

There are several stories regarding how war broke out in Manchukuo and the other parts of China. One story is, "the Japanese Kwantung Army went out of control." Another is, "the Chinese Communist Party actually planned it." Yet another is, "it happened because of the Chinese Nationalist Party Army." There are all sorts of stories, but we don't know the truth. Each side probably had a gripe with the other. Japan probably had both the idea of believing that this kind of expansionism was right and the idea that it was wrong.

However, if you look at it geopolitically, first off, you have the factor of Great Britain extending its rule all the way up to India. Maybe Nepal, too? Nepal was also taken, so if you look at the flow of things, there was strong reason to suspect that the West would begin to take control of China. At the point when the Qing Dynasty escaped into Manchukuo, the West probably would've carved up what was left of China.

I'm talking about the danger that almost happened after the Manchurian Incident but didn't. If Japan hadn't fought, things probably would've been like, "South of the Yangtze will belong to blah-blah" and, for example, "the area to the north of that will be U.S. territory." It would've been something like that.

SATOMURA:
Hmm. That's true.

KUNIO NAKAGAWA:
So, either way, the result would've been the same.

SATOMURA:
Right.

KUNIO NAKAGAWA:
Either way, they would've been put under colonial rule.

SATOMURA:
Yes.

Now, 70 years after the war, is the time to reassess History from the Manchurian Incident onward

OIKAWA:
At the beginning of this year, His Imperial Majesty spoke on his feelings regarding the new year and said something like, "This year marks 70 years since the end of WWII. I think now is the time to relearn history from the Manchurian Incident* onward."

You, Colonel Nakagawa, were actually involved with this. I think it's appropriate to assume the following: His Imperial Majesty is suggesting that we should look at this topic from a broader viewpoint, as you said, and that the history since the Manchurian Incident isn't simply a story of the military, or specifically the Kwantung Army, going out of control. What are your thoughts on this?

• SPIRITUAL INTERVIEW •

KUNIO NAKAGAWA:
Well, right now, His Imperial Majesty is not allowed to make political statements, so we can only guess at the true meaning of his words. In any case, I think it would've been possible for Japan to focus solely on protecting Manchukuo, but if internal warfare and conflict were to break out on many other parts of China, which was the larger expanse of land, we already knew that it would subsequently become a target for the West. We could already foresee that they would come from the Philippines to take Indonesia and even the southern part of China.

This is why the Allies established the ABCD encirclement[†]. They laid down an encirclement of economic sanctions and basically said, "We won't let a single drop of oil enter Japan."

SATOMURA:
Yes.

---

[*] The Manchurian Incident: a military confrontation in 1931 between Japan and China that sparked 15 years of war [Manchurian Incident, Second Sino-Japanese War and Greater East Asia War].

[†] ABCD encirclement: the name given to a coercive diplomatic strategy, mainly economic sanctions, used against Japan by America, Britain, China and the Netherlands [American-British-Chinese-Dutch]. The strategy was employed during WWII as a countermeasure to the advancement of Japanese forces into French Indochina. Also known as the ABCD Line.

KUNIO NAKAGAWA:

I think that you're having the same problem now. But the question here is, "What would happen if not even one drop of oil was allowed into Japan?" That would be quite a problem, wouldn't it?

Take the current situation. We're hearing reports saying that the depreciation of the yen will raise the fuel prices and others saying that they won't. This is all fine and well for places which can extract their own oil, such as the United States. But for a country like Japan which can't get its own oil, this kind of thing is just... We were an industrial nation by then, you know? We won't be able to run our industrial production like raw steel or iron. We won't be able to make ships. Our factories won't be able to produce. We won't be able to make aircrafts. So, this is a matter of life and death.

Also, regarding iron ore, Manchuria had it. Mainland China had things like coal, too. But by that time, we had already entered the age of petroleum. The thing about petroleum was that we were buying it mainly from the United States. I think we were buying about 70 to 80 percent of our petroleum from the U.S., which became our enemy in the war.

SATOMURA:

Yes, that's true.

KUNIO NAKAGAWA:
We were dependent on the U.S. for the majority of our fuel. So, the question was, "Can an industrial nation continue to function if that supply were to be stopped?" If that happened, then you simply have no choice but to go and take places that have oil supply. I think the Americans knew we would try to procure places in the south that had oil supply. Roosevelt was sly, so I imagine he already predicted this.

They formed the ABCD encirclement fully knowing that. So, actually, what they really wanted to do was to smack Japan down while going on to capture areas from Indochina up, including mainland China. I think they had that kind of ambition.

SATOMURA:
I see.

KUNIO NAKAGAWA:
They hid that ambition behind the false pretext of fighting to save that area from Japan. They used that pretext to make it seem like they were knights in shining armor.

The people of Palau are grateful to Japan For being able to prosper

SATOMURA:
Earlier, you said that there were many different opinions within Japan. It was unilaterally claimed at the subsequent Tokyo Trials, considering the chain of events from the Battle of Peleliu Island to the end of the Greater East Asia War, "Japan, and only Japan, attempted to expand throughout Asia under an aggressive policy. Japan acted under that kind of strategy."

That historical view has persisted, not only among overseas—particularly the Western world that originally proclaimed it—but even within the hearts and minds of the Japanese people. This view has continued up to the present day, 70 years after the end of the war.

KUNIO NAKAGAWA:
Yeah.

SATOMURA:
In a way, the statement that Prime Minister Murayama made in 1995 represented this. He basically admitted that the previous war was an invasion and said that Japan caused much trouble for the other countries of Asia. The Japanese people have been held captive by this viewpoint for ages. What are your thoughts on this?

KUNIO NAKAGAWA:
At that time, I believe the president of Palau was President Kuniwo Nakamura [see Figure 14], whose father was Japanese. As for Mr. Murayama, there was that time when he didn't go [to the Commemoration Ceremony for Palau's 1st Anniversary of Independence], which meant the Rising Sun Flag couldn't be raised. President Nakamura must've been extremely frustrated.

SATOMURA:
Ah.

KUNIO NAKAGAWA:
Representatives of countries from all around the world came, except for Japan. And when Japan made an apology saying, "We did bad things," I think President Kuniwo Nakamura asked, "What exactly did Japan do that was bad?" He picked up on the fact that the media coverage was off the mark and said, "Japan only tried to protect [Palau]. We're all thankful to the prosperity that Japan has brought us, so what do you have to apologize for?" [See Figure 15.]

If the people of China and the Korean Peninsula want to blame Japan for everything, I guess that's fine because that's their nature. But if it hadn't been for Japan, I'm sure that area would've been attacked and

Figure 14.

Kuniwo Nakamura [1943-present]: the 5th president of Palau [served Jan. 1993-Jan. 2001]. A man of Japanese descent. Nakamura placed importance on diplomacy and trade with Japan. Visited Japan repeatedly in the 1990s. He has also been visiting Japan frequently since leaving office.

Figure 15.

The 9th Palauan President Remengesau [serving since Jan. 2013] and Prime Minister Abe. The two talked in a commemoration of the 20th anniversary of the establishment of diplomatic relations between Japan and the Republic of Palau, on December 17, 2014.

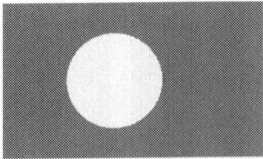

The flag of Palau
The yellow circle on a light blue background represents the blue expanse of the Pacific Ocean and the beautiful moon. Some say that the flag's similarity in design to Japan's rising sun flag expresses Palau's spirit of friendship toward Japan.

conquered by the U.S. and Russia. They [China and the Korean Peninsula] could establish independence because the U.S. and Russia attacked us under the claim, "Hey, Japan is the one who invaded." The two countries couldn't take the land for themselves, since they made that claim. That's probably how it all played out.

China and the USSR became communist countries As a result of the U.S. joining the war

KUNIO NAKAGAWA:
At the beginning of the Greater East Asia War, Japan entered the Tripartite Pact* with Germany and Italy in an attempt to halt the spread of the Communist Party. This resulted in the forming of the Axis Powers. But look at what happened after the war.

As a result of the U.S. joining the battle, the giant People's Republic of China adopted a Communist Party government. Also, Japan smashed the massive Russia in the Russo-Japanese War† and if the power relationship between countries had been handled well, Russia could've been a capitalist nation. But instead,

---

* The Tripartite Pact: an anti-communist, anti-Soviet agreement concluded between Japan, Germany and Italy from 1936 to 1937 in opposition to the global communist movement.

† The Russo-Japanese War: a war which was fought from February 1904 to September 1905, between Empire of Japan and Russian Empire.

revolution broke out again. After that, the Communist Bloc was formed because USSR emerged as a victorious nation in WWII. Then the Cold War lasted for many years. Numerous people were purged domestically, which is something you all aren't aware of.

SATOMURA:
Right.

KUNIO NAKAGAWA:
One of the basic precepts of communism is, "revolution by arms." The communist way of thinking is to continually instigate purging and do whatever it takes to succeed, even if that means sending people who get in the way to political imprisonment or even executing them. Their idea is to completely annihilate the enemy. There isn't even a hint of humanitarianism in this.

This type of thinking ended up controlling the giant land masses of China and the USSR. So, you have to ask yourselves, was the U.S. support in this region actually beneficial, after all? Has the postwar layout of world powers in the past several decades been the correct flow of history? I really want people to think about this thoroughly.

SATOMURA:
OK.

KUNIO NAKAGAWA:

The truth is, if the U.S. had cooperated with Japan in order to guide those people, they probably would've been able to build a better country. But the U.S. just couldn't help but think of us as the enemy. In the end, it was the Americans' racist viewpoint that led them to see us as their enemy.

There was this widespread, deep-rooted belief, "We can't allow Japan to become the leader of the yellow race on behalf of the white race, because the yellow race is inferior race to us." I think so.

• FOR THE LOVE OF THE COUNTRY •

5

Colonel Nakagawa Refutes the Lies of Nanking Massacre and Military Comfort Women

The Nanking Massacre is unthinkable considering The Japanese military DNA

AYAORI:
The Nanking Incident* [Nanking Massacre] was acknowledged during the Tokyo Trials. Today, the general opinion is that the Japanese army was an atrocious military force, with the Nanking Massacre serving as a symbol of that. How do you see this, from the viewpoint of someone who actually served in the Chinese battlefield?

KUNIO NAKAGAWA:
Well, I served in the 14th division, which was under the command of the Kwantung Army, so I did know a bit about China. You know, if the Japanese military was the kind of organization that would just go in and

---

* Nanking incident: an incident in 1937 in which Japanese troops are said to have massacred 300,000 Chinese upon capturing the city of Nanking. However, a number of doubts have been raised regarding the authenticity of this account.

massacre 300,000 civilians, then we wouldn't have gone to Palau and made all the islanders on Peleliu Island evacuate to prevent them from dying. All our military divisions had this DNA. So, doing that kind of a thing is simply unthinkable.

AYAORI:
Right. That's true.

KUNIO NAKAGAWA:
If we were such people, we probably would've used them as human shields. What I mean is, if the Japanese army was that kind of an organization, we would've gathered up all the Palau islanders and lined them up as human shields along the coastline [*stretches arms out horizontally*].

SATOMURA:
True.

KUNIO NAKAGAWA:
We would've done so in order to tell everyone that the U.S. massacred the people of Palau. Probably.

AYAORI:
In fact, not a single person from Palau died.

KUNIO NAKAGAWA:
Exactly.

"Please report the full names of the people who Died in Nanking"

KUNIO NAKAGAWA:
In Nanking, there were no civilian victims. I mean, there probably were some troubles or small conflicts, yes. But, you know, Japan held "military versus military" as its most basic way of thinking. There simply was no concept of fighting non-military groups.

Of course, we couldn't trust people who disguised themselves as civilians and sniped at us. We couldn't let our guard down against the snipers, so yes, the Japanese army may have shot at some of these kinds of people. But in general, that kind of thing didn't happen.

SATOMURA:
I see.

KUNIO NAKAGAWA:
If they're going to make such a claim as a nation, then they should be able to say how many people actually died because they must've had family registry for the

city called Nanking. I want them to release the specific names.

SATOMURA:
Right.

KUNIO NAKAGAWA:
Survivors must've returned alive. So, who died?

AYAORI:
I see.

KUNIO NAKAGAWA:
Japan knows who died in the Tokyo Air Raids. We know who died when the atomic bomb was dropped on Hiroshima. This is how the Japanese government is able to pay pension money to the survivors. We have that information for Nagasaki, too. We know such information, even when people die in the scale of hundreds of thousands. We know who died. Because those records exist. If they're going to say, "You killed 300,000 people," I want them to show us the records of the names. Who died?

AYAORI:
The truth, however, is that this information is being hidden. Even the simple act of researching it is, in fact, forbidden.

KUNIO NAKAGAWA:
Well, you know, they have a different purpose... Ultimately, it's just like Hitler's policy of Aryan race dominance* and the plan to discriminate against and massacre the Jewish people. I'm saying that the Chinese government today is trying to do this very same thing.

I mean, they're making claims like, "The Chinese people are the elders in terms of culture and Chinese culture is responsible for every part of Japanese growth and development. But after all of that, these cocky Japanese had the nerve to actually attack and invade China. This is completely unforgivable." They label us as "a cruel race." This kind of talk is, from my perspective as a soldier, nothing more than an excuse to occupy Japan. Or, at the very least, an excuse to attack.

SATOMURA:
I agree.

KUNIO NAKAGAWA:
From the viewpoint of a soldier, that is. China is a permanent member of the UN, right? Its [China's] true intention seems to be to mandate Japan.

SATOMURA:
I see.

The issue of military comfort women is Absolutely ridiculous!

SATOMURA:

In that context, we see that China is taking advantage of this year [2015] being the 70th anniversary since the end of WWII. China is attempting to register, as a UNESCO Memory of the World, material related to the Nanking Massacre or material related to the existence of military comfort women[†] who were allegedly abducted mainly from the Korean Peninsula and forced into sexual slavery by the Japanese military.

KUNIO NAKAGAWA:
Yeah.

SATOMURA:
This could be seen as an attempt to establish those things as historical facts. How do you see this?

---

[*] Policy of Aryan dominance: a government policy based on the belief of Hitler, the leader of Nazi Germany during WWII. Hitler believed that the Aryan people are the sole legitimate people of Germany. Theoretically, this way of thinking supported the expulsion of other races, such as the Jews.

[†] Military comfort women: South Korea is claiming that the Japanese army forcibly collected 200,000 Korean women to serve as "sex slaves" during WWII. At the time, there were private brothels near army posts like other countries, but there is no concrete proof that the Japanese Army was involved in the forcible act.

KUNIO NAKAGAWA:

Japan annexed Korea. Koreans and Japanese people received equal treatment. Some Koreans had Japanese surnames as well, so you couldn't necessary tell if a woman was either Korean or Japanese. Of course, it's true that there were inns near military divisions bound for the frontlines that would take care of them. So, there were even people who offered that kind of recreation. If they were doing that as a business, then that's their own choice; they can't complain. But if women were packed into trucks and brought along forcibly by the military, as if they were soldiers being drafted, then that would've been quite an inhumane act, although not as inhumane as what Nazis did. This is probably where the Chinese claims come from.

However, what we do know from our own experience or, at the very least, what I know from watching the Kwantung Army is that... I mean, OK, having men be alone or single for many years is a difficult thing and can cause problems. They were strictly forbidden from entering civilian residences to rape and plunder because such acts violate military regulations. So, I believe that there was some sort of system to allow the troops a chance to play as long as they paid for it. I mean, there may have been professional women, who received fair payment, serving them. That's entirely possible.

• Spiritual Interview •

However, it was strictly forbidden to kidnap civilians and rape and plunder like monsters. You would surely be locked away in military prison. I mean, such acts were looked upon as very serious offenses.

So, as a person who was in a position of authority, I must say, "It's absolutely ridiculous to think that the military could've perpetuated or knowingly allowed this sort of conduct!"

SATOMURA:
I see.

KUNIO NAKAGAWA:
Obviously, we can't completely rule out the possibility that some traders may have recruited these kinds of women by asking, "Do you want to make some money?" and bringing them to the military areas. But at the very least, it's absolutely untrue that the military forced women into being sex slaves at gunpoint!

China and South Korea's frustration over not Winning independence

SATOMURA:
How do you feel about the Japanese government and the people of Japan who don't take a stand against this

kind of Chinese and Korean propaganda?

KUNIO NAKAGAWA:
The fact that they're making those sorts of propaganda is nothing more than the flip side of their frustration—frustration over not winning their independence through their own military victories. South Korea didn't gain its own independence by counterattacking and pushing Japanese forces back.

SATOMURA:
Right.

KUNIO NAKAGAWA:
Right? So, there's frustration behind this.

SATOMURA:
Yes.

KUNIO NAKAGAWA:
Actually, Koreans participated in killing a lot of "southern dojin [natives]," if I were to use their term. They went to the southern front as soldiers in the Japanese army. By no means did we ever attempt to massacre any natives, but the propaganda that they put out claims, "Japan did this." The thing is, though, if that were true, then it would also be true that the people

of the Korean Peninsula also went in and killed lots of their fellow Asians. Isn't that right?

As for China, I don't recall our forces actually fighting Mao Zedong's Chinese Communist Party government.

SATOMURA:
Right.

KUNIO NAKAGAWA:
We didn't fight those people. What happened was they just had all sorts of internal fighting and conflicts. Those people were always on the run. They quickly gained power only after WWII ended.

SATOMURA:
True.

KUNIO NAKAGAWA:
I don't recall fighting them at all. So, they can't claim they won over Japan. We weren't defeated by them, either. The question is, why were they left free to do what they wanted? There's a suspicion that Franklin D. Roosevelt may have been a communist.

SATOMURA & AYAORI:
Indeed.

KUNIO NAKAGAWA:

At the very least, we do know that there was a USSR spy* among his close advisors. I believe Churchill and Roosevelt had a discussion in which they agreed, "We can't win WWII without having USSR as our ally." I think that's how things went.

---

* USSR spy: Harry Dexter White [1892–1948] was a government official for the United States of America. He served as an assistant to Secretary of the Treasury Henry Morgenthau, Jr. under the Franklin Delano Roosevelt administration. The fact that White served as a spy for the USSR Comintern has been confirmed in Venona Project documents.

6

Colonel Nakagawa's Way to Protect The Current Japan from China

Japan must become a deterrent to keep China in check

AYAORI:

The Chinese Communist Party is attempting to swallow the Pacific Ocean using military means. This is threatening Nansei-shoto [southwestern islands off Kyusyu], as well as Okinawa. How should Japan confront this as seen from your viewpoint as a military official? Also, how should we protect our own soil? What are your thoughts on these issues?

KUNIO NAKAGAWA:

Well, China's already building a stronghold on the Spratly Islands, right? China has built up the coral reef area to several dozens of times its size and already started constructing a fort there. There's a navy base being built there, right?* [See Figure 16.]

---

* It has been reported that, as of February 2015, China is proceeding with a large-scale reclamation on three shore reefs in the Spratly Islands.

SATOMURA:
Yes, there is.

KUNIO NAKAGAWA:
So, it's clear that China has the intent to occupy. It's taking its surrounding areas.

SATOMURA:
Yes.

Figure 16.

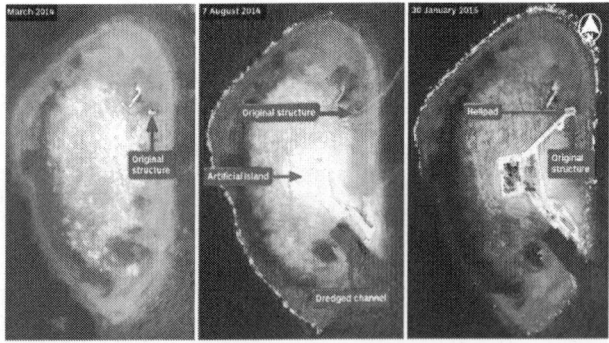

Satellite images showing the process of China's effective control over one of the islands in the Spratly Islands [*Jane's Defence Weekly News*, February 15, 2015]. The islands, located in the South China Sea, are the subject of territorial disputes between countries such as Vietnam and the Philippines. There were originally only a few small concrete foundations, but now there is an artificial island featuring a helipad, a runway, a seaport and a large-scale barracks.

KUNIO NAKAGAWA:

Another thing is, Okinawa should... Japan... You know, the Battle of Okinawa had a tragic end to it, so I can understand that there's a very good reason for the people of Okinawa to dislike the U.S. forces. I can completely understand that feeling. Even so, they need to know that the base for a Chinese invasion is on Hainan Island.

Hainan Island is very close to Taiwan. China is currently constructing things like submarines and will next construct a fleet led by an aircraft carrier. Right now, Okinawa is the bothersome issue. Taiwan and Okinawa are the areas of concern. If China takes Taiwan, next would be Okinawa. If China takes these two areas, Taiwan and Okinawa, the Chinese navy would be able to do anything.

China wants to take this area in the South China Sea and also wants to establish the Chinese version of Japan's "Greater East Asia Co-Prosperity Sphere*." China even wants to take Hawaii, so it's indeed the Greater East Asia Co-Prosperity Sphere. This is what China is trying to do right now.

The question is, "Who would be able to oppose

---

* Greater East Asia Co-Prosperity Sphere: a plan Japan had during WWII. The plan was to establish a sphere of a new world order in East and Southeast Asia, with Japan as the leader, for the sake of coexistence and co-prosperity of the region. The plan also intended to liberate those regions from Western countries—mainly Great Britain and the United States.

this?" What you have to understand is, the other nations of Asia don't share the same public opinion and ideas, about what's right and wrong, that you all [Japanese people] have cultivated since the end of the war. In fact, you could even say that they want Japan to serve as a breakwater. So, at the very least, you must be a deterrent to keep China in check.

And with a president like President Obama who just keeps retreating over and over again, expanding conflict in many different areas, the U.S. is no longer of any help. I'm completely fine with ending the era of a world that revolves around the U.S., of course, but if it falls, we'll be the next to be invaded. History of other racial groups within China tells us they were invaded, so this whole thing of China invading us under the belief that China is right is something that we know will keep happening, over and over again. I definitely think China will do exactly the things that the Japanese forces didn't do.

SATOMURA:
OK.

Japan's basic goal was "Coexistence and co-prosperity"

KUNIO NAKAGAWA:
Just as the name "Greater East Asia Co-Prosperity Sphere" implies, Japan was basically seeking coexistence and co-prosperity. Of course, there may have been some [locals] who were unwilling and I can't say that we didn't make unjust demands for supplies and food. But in general, we intended to cooperate and prosper together.

That's how things actually were in Palau. We actualized coexistence and co-prosperity, gave them the kind of education they hadn't received before, built hospitals, built roads and constructed a lot of infrastructure. I'm sure the same thing happened in Taiwan.

SATOMURA:
I see.

KUNIO NAKAGAWA:
So, basically, we wanted to make life better for the locals, too.

AYAORI:
Right.

KUNIO NAKAGAWA:
We didn't go there intending to exploit the area. In contrast, if you look at India, it didn't improve at all even though Great Britain ruled there for 150 years. India became even more poor. The British exploited it.

SATOMURA:
Yes.

KUNIO NAKAGAWA:
Right? Sugar, tea, textiles... they just exploited all sorts of things. That's all. So, when you really look at what happened, I think you can see that we [Japan] had a fundamentally different approach [from the West]. We thought of the locals as fellow Asians.

If the Japan-U.S. alliance is cut off, Okinawa will become a Chinese territory

KUNIO NAKAGAWA:
You know, this frustration of China and Korea, this frustration over not winning against us in battle... In terms of South Korea, this is apparent in the issues surrounding Takeshima*. Recently, I think there was a "Takeshima Day" [Feb. 22], but you know, it was South Korea who occupied Takeshima after the

• SPIRITUAL INTERVIEW •

Greater East Asia War. This is a historical fact. Everyone knows it. Everybody knows, but no one says it.

Japan no longer has a military... We don't have one under the new constitution. We've completely "renounced war as means of settling international disputes." This allowed them to take Takeshima, the very example of their desire to steal Japanese territory to their heart's content, correct? I mean, it's very easy to take land from a country with no military to protect it. China hasn't been able to do much of that, but is itching for that kind of a chance.

Basically speaking, it [China] also has atomic bombs... I mean, nuclear missiles. So, there's absolutely no way we could win in an all-out war. The minute China throws humanitarianism out the window, we've lost. We know this.

We're fine as long as the Japan-U.S. alliance holds up, but China is most certainly attempting to drive a wedge in that. The very second the Japan-U.S. alliance falls apart, Okinawa will become a Chinese territory.

---

* Takeshima: a group of islets in the southwestern part of Japan Sea. Former South Korean President Syngman Rhee unilaterally claimed sovereignty over the islets and sent his military there in 1953, when Japan still hadn't formed JSDF [Japan Self-Defense Forces]. South Korea has been illegally occupying Takeshima ever since.

SATOMURA:
From your viewpoint as someone who fought the U.S. on Peleliu Island, do you feel that we absolutely mustn't let go of the Japan-U.S. alliance?

KUNIO NAKAGAWA:
There's no other choice if you're going to protect Japan via the status quo. There's no other way. We're completely surrounded by countries that possess nuclear weapons. Another option is India. But even if you asked India to fire nuclear weapons at places that are invading Japan, we don't know for sure whether India will do so.

China's national policy of trying to deceive Japan

OIKAWA:
A few moments ago, Master Okawa touched on this in his pre-interview explanation, but about five years ago, a U.S. TV station made a documentary drama called *The Pacific* that covered the Pacific Ocean battlefront. Three out of the total of ten episodes dealt with the Battle of Peleliu Island.

In other words, unfortunately, right now Americans probably know more about the Battle of Peleliu Island and Colonel Nakagawa than we, the Japanese, do.

KUNIO NAKAGAWA:
Yeah, I know.

OIKAWA:
This year marks 70 years after the end of war. What would you like Americans to see if they were to look back on this historical event once more?

KUNIO NAKAGAWA:
As things stand right now, the U.S. will come into some kind of military conflict with China at some point. The U.S. and China will clash. Whether that will center around the Spratly Islands, Taiwan, Okinawa or farther south than that, is still unknown.

Now, Chinese fishing boats are haughtily sailing all the way into waters around the Ogasawara Islands [also known as the Bonin Islands] to take coral as if they own the area. Furthermore, recently, Chinese people have been buying huge quantities of goods in the Ginza area during the Chinese New Year season to take back to China. So, they're already starting to look at us as a colony under Chinese rule.

They're doing this on purpose. They're trying to show us that Chinese money will set the Japanese economy right. The Chinese government is encouraging the wealthy Chinese to come to Japan and buy things. By doing so, the government is conveying the message to Japan, "If you don't keep building factories in China and expand your scope of trade with China, you won't be long." China is doing this as a national policy.

SATOMURA:
National policy?

KUNIO NAKAGAWA:
Yes, as a national policy. Spending money [in Japan] to show just how much money China has. This is what the Chinese are doing. We're in a war of intelligence; a war to see if we'll be deceived by this or not.

Energy development vital for Japan

KUNIO NAKAGAWA:
So, you see, we have things like the anti-U.S. movement in Okinawa and the movement to abolish nuclear power in Japan, including feelings about the recent nuclear radiation problem. But do you know who's really enjoying all of this? China, of course. If Japan did away with nuclear power, it would no longer be an industrial nation.

Right now, most of our oil comes from the Persian Gulf. Hainan Island, which was mentioned earlier, is home to China's largest naval port. The Chinese navy takes off from there. If Taiwan falls... If China annexes Taiwan, then oil from the west would stop coming in [to Japan]. Just like the ABCD encirclement, oil would stop coming into the country.

If that happens, the only option would be to detour around to the south. Here, China already has influence in the Philippines and is now trying to get its hands on Australia. Even so, Australia started to notice this and is finally starting to adjust its policies. Vietnam is changing its policy, too. Places like Thailand and Cambodia are starting to think, "If we don't change and start siding with Japan, things are going to get dangerous." So, an ideological battle is under way right now.

In other words, if we can't get oil from the south either, Japan will be in terrible danger. Therefore, the only way we'll be able to survive is to develop a semi-permanent energy source like the Fast Breeder Reactor Monju[*], which is currently non-operational. There's no other way. You could put up those solar panels, but all it takes is one airstrike and that would be the end of everything. That type of thing doesn't help generate power at all.

---

[*] Fast Breeder Reactor Monju: a fast breeder reactor [FBR] located in Fukui, Japan. An FBR is a specialized nuclear reactor that uses plutonium as fuel to generate more power than it takes to operate.

7

My Wish is for Our People to Regain Their Japanese Pride

**"The Japanese people who fought and died
Have been praying for the prosperity of Japan"**

AYAORI:
Considering this year marks 70 years since the end of the war, issues revolving around history are definitely important, but at the same time, commemorating the people who lost their lives is also important. His Imperial Majesty plans to visit Peleliu Island to commemorate them.

KUNIO NAKAGAWA:
Yeah, that's right.

AYAORI:
What are the people who actually lost their lives on Peleliu Island or the people who lost their lives on other frontlines doing right now? What do they want from the Japanese people of today?

KUNIO NAKAGAWA:
Well, they've all been praying for the prosperity of Japan.

AYAORI:
Ah... I see.

KUNIO NAKAGAWA:
So, basically they are saying, "Don't let our deaths be in vain." Of course, a lot of them have been reborn [on earth]. I mean, it's already been 70 years since.

SATOMURA:
Ah... Is that so?

KUNIO NAKAGAWA:
Yes.

Most of the Japanese soldiers who died on Peleliu Island have returned to Heaven

SATOMURA:
Here's something I believe is extremely important when thinking about right and wrong from a spiritual viewpoint. Basically, the U.S. and the other nations who won in WWII are saying, "Justice was on our

side. This was a battle fought between the side of God and the side of the devil. And the fascists or devil's fascism lost."

If what they're saying is true, then for example, the Japanese soldiers who fought on Peleliu Island must've gone to Hell while the soldiers on the U.S. side, which ultimately won the war, must've gone to Heaven. What happened to you and your men after dying on Peleliu Island?

KUNIO NAKAGAWA:
Obviously, a lot of that depends on the individual. Everyone has his own level of belief and goes to Heaven or Hell depending on that. The same thing happened with the U.S. troops. Americans have a tendency to think of everyone who was killed in a war as a hero, but the truth is, not everyone was taken up to God as a hero. I believe there were many people who died with hatred in their hearts and many people who died in sadness.

SATOMURA:
Yes.

KUNIO NAKAGAWA:
Both sides... I mean, it's true that a type of Hell is formed after a battle. But as time passes, it gets calmer.

• SPIRITUAL INTERVIEW •

Just as muddy water turns clear, the top layer turns pure, little by little, and starts to separate. The bottom becomes filled with things that sink and the top becomes clear. Whether a person goes to the top or the bottom varies for each individual.

So, there are two types of people. One is, people who died fighting, from their heart, for love and to protect their homeland and families. The other is, people who had no thoughts of their own and only followed orders—these people are lost. Not to mention, there are people who suffered because they starved to death and are, therefore, lost. There are people who suffered in such materialistic sense, specifically food provision.

As of right now, out of the 10,000 or so people who died... Hmm, let's see. I mean, there's no way I can look up each person like taking a census, but I believe about 7,000 out of the 10,000 or so people who died have gone up to the heavenly world.

SATOMURA:
Ah...

KUNIO NAKAGAWA:
I guess there are about 3,000 people who are suffering for now. Anyhow, out of the 7,000 or so souls who returned to the heavenly world, about half of them

have been reborn in Japan once again.

SATOMURA:
Ah! I see.

KUNIO NAKAGAWA:
They're already living their lives again in the postwar era. That's how things are. But I plan on following up with the others.

Japanese soldiers will be treated as heroes

KUNIO NAKAGAWA:
There were a lot of people who were designated as "Class A" war criminals of WWII and executed. For example, people like General Tomoyuki Yamashita, who was known as "the Tiger of Malaya," were definitely hero material. He was a hero. What he did were acts of a hero. And I think he'll be remembered as such.

Even the poem of Nimitz is engraved into the monument on Peleliu Island.* You know, the Battle of, um...

---

*Words inscribed on the epitaph:

> TOURISTS FROM EVERY COUNTRY WHO VISIT THIS ISLAND SHOULD BE TOLD HOW COURAGEOUS AND PATRIOTIC WERE THE JAPANESE SOLDIERS WHO ALL DIED DEFENDING THIS ISLAND

SATOMURA:
Battle of Thermopylae?

KUNIO NAKAGAWA:
Yeah, yeah, that. That's it.

SATOMURA:
That famous standoff between Sparta and Persia?

KUNIO NAKAGAWA:
Yeah. That [Battle of Thermopylae] in which 300 Spartan warriors fought against a giant force of over 65,000 troops and were defeated. Americans made a memorial there that speaks of us in those terms. It says something along the lines of, "Tourists, take note. Know that heroes rest here." People will probably come to find this sort of thing even more.

Through things like the Vietnam War and the Iraq War, even the U.S. is really starting to realize that there's no such thing as a war that's completely just. People thought that the Iraq War was for a just cause, but look at it now in terms of what has happened since. You have to ask, how many people died as a result of events that unfolded after the fall of the Hussein regime? And how many people are still dying now? These are just starting to come to light.

So, people have to understand that a cause can't be

called just if it doesn't consider the differences in religion, culture, race or ethnicity.

SATOMURA:
I see.

The Emperor's visit to Peleliu Island is a blessing

SATOMURA:
Earlier, you said that about 70 percent of the soldiers returned to the heavenly world. Are those souls going to Yasukuni first?

KUNIO NAKAGAWA:
Well, there are some who were able to go and some who weren't even aware that they were allowed to go to Yasukuni. But, you know, His Majesty plans to visit Peleliu Island... Well, it's not like the souls of the fallen reside in their bones or anything. But his feelings, the message that he acknowledges our service, will definitely be heard by everyone.

SATOMURA:
I see. Then, his visit will be a very important event for them?

KUNIO NAKAGAWA:
It's a blessing. Something to truly be grateful for. The only thing that would make us happier is if Emperor Showa were to come. If he were to tell us, "You did well," we'd be even happier.

AYAORI:
A total of several million Japanese troops died. Are you saying that about 70 percent of those troops returned to the heavenly world?

KUNIO NAKAGAWA:
The death count including civilians was about 3 million, right? The population of Japan at that time was about 80 million or 85 million... Anyway, somewhere a little over 80 million. We were saying *ichioku gyokusai* [literally "100 million shattered jewels," a wartime slogan meant to motivate 100 million people to give their lives in honorable suicide attacks], but the population must've actually been somewhere around 80 million. This population has increased to somewhere around 120 million people. So, our efforts have definitely paid off through the postwar prosperity of Japan.

I'm indeed concerned about where our country is headed, but I believe the people's views on these things will change when history changes. The U.S. is in the process of accumulating experience. The U.S.

will experience similar situations in Okinawa, Taiwan and the Philippines.

SATOMURA:
I see.

Asking about Colonel Kunio Nakagawa's Last moments and his post-death experiences

AYAORI:
I'm also very interested in hearing about your last moments. There are many different stories as to how you died, including one that says you committed suicide and another that says you died facing off against U.S. troops in battle. What actually happened? Also, what happened after that [after death]?

KUNIO NAKAGAWA:
We didn't have any food or water left. We were all out of ammunition, too. So, in the end, I took my Japanese sword and slashed my enemies.

AYAORI:
Is that so?

KUNIO NAKAGAWA:
Yeah. I slashed through them. It was a surprise night raid. We made a night raid. We set out on a night raid, but at that time I was severely wounded, so I couldn't really fight anymore. Therefore, just like Takamori Saigo*, at a certain point I decided, "All right, this is enough" and committed *seppuku*, with someone assisting to behead me. That's how I died.

SATOMURA:
Ah, I see...

AYAORI:
After that, did you return to the heavenly world without any trouble? Or did you stay on earth for a while, out of a sense of obligation?

KUNIO NAKAGAWA:
We were in the middle of a battle, so it's true that I didn't leave the island right away. But you can assume I returned to the heavenly world, at least by the end of the war.

---

* The end of Takamori Saigo: Takamori Saigo [1828-1877] was a Japanese military official, politician and one of the key figures of the Meiji Restoration. He later turned against the new Meiji government and led fellow former samurais who held frustration toward it through the Seinan War [Satsuma Rebellion]. Saigo and his forces were ultimately surrounded by the government forces. After being shot himself, Saigo told one of his subordinates, "I've had enough" and had the subordinate behead him.

AYAORI:
The name General Yamashita came up earlier. Is he with you in the heavenly world?

KUNIO NAKAGAWA:
Yeah. They've all returned to the heavenly world.

AYAORI:
Oh, OK.

KUNIO NAKAGAWA:
So, what was judged as "evil" after the war doesn't coincide with the Judgment of God.

AYAORI:
I see. As one example of a famous person at the time, there's General Hitoshi Imamura, the man who ruled Indonesia. Is he with you in the heavenly world?

KUNIO NAKAGAWA:
As for each person, I think you should ask individually. I don't think I should be the one to talk about such things.

• SPIRITUAL INTERVIEW •

"Thinking that we didn't die in vain is
The best memorial service for us"

KUNIO NAKAGAWA:

Well, not everyone went up to the heavenly world. There were probably people who died blaming themselves, who also felt immense responsibility over what happened and still remain there. But the majority of the souls are aware that they are already dead, since they fought knowing the existence of a soul and the afterlife.

I imagine that some of the souls have reached Yasukuni, but the problem is that Yasukuni has no effect. Honestly speaking, it doesn't have much effect. Truth be told. Intervention by foreign countries has led to a humiliating situation where our prime ministers can't visit Yasukuni, even though it's a shrine so close to the Prime Minister's Official Residence. And this situation has persisted for 70 years now. During this whole time, we've had to say that our self-defense forces aren't the military. So, Yasukuni's effect to purify spirits is extremely weak.

That's why, if the Japanese people today would properly acknowledge that we died for... I mean, the fallen are all treated like heroes in the United States. If you would do that for us, I think a lot of souls would feel peace of mind. There are indeed some souls who are bound to the time of the battle, so the true memorial service for us would be for everyone to feel that the battle we fought and our deaths were not in vain. That would be the best memorial service for us.

SATOMURA:

In other words, that battle actually meant a lot in terms of protecting our home country and families, right?

KUNIO NAKAGAWA:

It's a very important thing. Take wars of the past. In Europe, for example, in religious wars between groups like the Protestants and the Catholics, they fought until the populations of their countries were reduced to one-third or even one-fourth. But this [Pacific War] didn't go as far. Three million Japanese people died, but eighty million people survived. This was the result of us putting up such a strong fight.

We were also able to preserve the Imperial system, so this is something to be very thankful for. But I would also like to go one step further and ask our people to regain their Japanese pride.

• SPIRITUAL INTERVIEW •

8

Where is Colonel Nakagawa Right Now?

Colonel Nakagawa is in a world of war gods with Spirits like Masashige Kusunoki

SATOMURA:
Where do you reside in the Spirit World right now? What kind of people are you with?

KUNIO NAKAGAWA:
"What kind of people," you ask? Hmm. I'm in a place similar to where spirits like Masashige Kusunoki [see Preface] are.

SATOMURA:
So, in that case, would it be correct to assume that you're close to the Japanese Spirit World, somewhere like *Takamagahara**?

KUNIO NAKAGAWA:
Umm... Well, where I am is a world of war gods, actually.

---

*Takamagahara: a higher spirit realm in Shintoism where Japanese gods reside.

AYAORI:
Earlier, Master Ryuho Okawa mentioned the name, Yukimura Sanada [see Chapter 1]. Do you have any connections to him?

KUNIO NAKAGAWA:
There's no direct connection, but I'm close to where he is.

SATOMURA:
You're close?

KUNIO NAKAGAWA:
Yeah, I guess you could say we're in the same sort of place...

AYAORI:
Did you fight together in the Osaka Winter Campaign and Summer Campaign*?

KUNIO NAKAGAWA:
Um... Well, that kind of... Wait a minute, are you all trying to identify and rate my past life?

---

*Osaka Winter Campaign and Summer Campaign: two battles initiated by the Tokugawa clan, who set up the Edo Bakufu [Edo government], in order to crush the Toyotomi clan, who had the former authority over Japan. The battles took place in the winter of 1614 and the summer of 1615.

• SPIRITUAL INTERVIEW •

SATOMURA:

No, we're not rating you. We just want to know what kind of reincarnation the soul of a hero goes through. We want to make that information available to future generations.

KUNIO NAKAGAWA:

You know, Japan actually has lots of war gods. I mean, war gods have been protecting Japan, that's how this small country has managed to remain independent for 3,000 years. In that sense, we believe that we served as shields for the 100 million people of Japan. "We won't have any regrets, even if we are to be crushed in our service as a shield." That's how we felt.

I was never anyone famous, but I probably did fight several times in the past as strategist-type commanders.

In his past lives, he fought and fell to protect Something great

SATOMURA:

For example, let's take your words "strategist-type commanders." If we replace "mainland Japan" with "Osaka Castle," there was a person who served as both a tactician and a commander; a man named Matabei Goto, who came out of the Kuroda clan. Do you have any connections to him?

KUNIO NAKAGAWA:
Umm... I'm not him, to be exact. Well, you could put it this way. Umm... All sorts of people serve during a war. People fulfill all sorts of roles in all sorts of places, so someone like me who was defeated and committed suicide in war shouldn't mention big names.

Anyhow, I died as a garrison commander, so I'd be relieved if you could just think that I was such type of people in the past, too.

SATOMURA:
It's just like you to be so humble. I guess you mean to say that you don't feel it's right to talk about this.

KUNIO NAKAGAWA:
Basically, you could say that I'm one of those people who have experienced that kind of a fight in the past, several times, in order to protect something very important and ended up falling. At times, I was one of the many who fought and fell to protect the shogun family. At other times, for a *daimyo*. And yet other times, for the emperor.

You know, I don't think it's a very good idea for someone who fell with 10,000 others in war to try and broadcast his own name to future generations in a bold way. So, I'd like to refrain from doing so.

SATOMURA:
Sure thing.

"I feel it's my responsibility to save as many troops As I can, down to the very last man"

SATOMURA:
So, let's change our viewpoint a bit now. You seem to have quite a bit of knowledge about modern times as well. Have you been watching all this time from the heavenly world? Also, you mentioned that out of the 7,000 people who returned to the heavenly world, about half of them have been reborn. What about yourself?

KUNIO NAKAGAWA:
Well, I mean, you know, after commanding and having my soldiers be killed on such huge scale, and being responsible for all of that, I just can't bring myself to be reborn until every single soul is saved. I feel it's my responsibility to save as many troops as I can, down to the very last man. I want to save their souls. I'm a war god, but at the same time, I'm also

serving the role of an angel who saves souls.

Putting me in the same class as the deities enshrined in places like the Nogi Shrine or Togo Shrine* is just... You know, they became gods because they won. There are things in the heavenly world which are similar to those kinds of shrines and there's actually a Kunio Nakagawa Shrine in the heavenly world. [*Laughs.*] There's no shrine for me in this world, but there is in the other world.

SATOMURA:
We feel that this spiritual message will help start one in this world.

---

* Nogi and Togo: both Maresuke Nogi [1849-1912] and Heihachiro Togo [1848-1934] were Japanese heroes during the Russo-Japanese War. Nogi was an army general and Togo a navy admiral. They are worshiped as gods in their respective shrines.

• SPIRITUAL INTERVIEW •

9

Break Free from Materialism and Revolutionize the Times

The bottom line is, "There's more to life than the one on earth"

KUNIO NAKAGAWA:
But, you know, I would appreciate it if some kind of *torii* [gateway entrance to a Shinto shrine] can be built on Peleliu Island. I would like to have a shrine be built there.

SATOMURA:
There apparently is a monument there [see Figure 17], but I believe you're speaking of ones that have some kind of object of faith.

Figure 17.

Peleliu Shrine [Nanko Shrine] that was constructed in 1934. People have been praying for the prosperity of the island at this shrine. The main deity worshiped there is Amaterasu-O-Mikami [Sun Goddess]. The souls of more than 10,000 soldiers who died in the Battle of Peleliu are enshrined here.

KUNIO NAKAGAWA:
There really is a strong element of materialistic thinking in all of this. The materialistic idea of "life in this world is all there is" has infested an ever-growing belief that the entire goal of life is only to live as long as possible, to save people using medical science, to save people by giving them food or, to say, "We want peace at all costs. We don't mind whether there's evil. It's better to not resist that and to just live as long as possible." This type of thinking really is on the rise.

The bottom line is, "There is more to life than the one on earth." We live an eternal life. We merely come down to earth in order to gain some kind of job experience or soul experience. This is where we learn about good and evil. This is where we learn about wisdom. This is where we learn about the difference between angels and devils. This is where we learn about the difference between loving people and hating people.

For your information, I don't hate the U.S. troops. The truth is, I have a desire to commemorate the Americans who died on Peleliu Island as well. They see us, who died an honorable death, as heroes, in their own way. In that sense, they have a fair mentality as military soldiers.

But what I want to say is that the feelings and vibrations coming from Japan are extremely weak. I really want our people to be strong.

Japan must work to get a higher level of Authority and respect

SATOMURA:
There's one last thing I would like to ask you. This year marks 70 years since the end of the war. Recently, there was a Japanese hostage incident within ISIL [Islamic State of Iraq and the Levant]. In Japan, many people were saying things like "the safety of life is paramount" and "life is the most important thing." Of course, life is definitely very important. But I feel that the belief of "without life, there's nothing you can do" is spreading throughout Japan, in this recent trend which you described as materialistic.

With that in mind, and also considering Prime Minister Abe who is saying, "I will issue a statement this year, which is the 70th year after WWII," is there anything you would like to say to the modern people of Japan?

KUNIO NAKAGAWA:
Well, first off, Prime Minister Abe is getting quite distracted by worldly matters. There are a lot of small attacks going on in terms of this world and he's getting

distracted by those. Attacks and counters from the left wing are pretty strong.

I understand, of course. I really do understand the view, "As long as we criticize the government, as long as we attack in a way that can't be ignored, they [the government] won't do bad things." I really understand that sort of view that assumes all people are basically evil in nature. It's also a fact that you could fail if you have too much confidence. So, I can completely see how some people would think that the entire nation shouldn't change based on his ideas alone.

But the thing is, it really is time for that kind of thing to happen. Obviously, we shouldn't rely solely on Abe himself, but I do think that no matter who the prime minister may be, Japan must become a nation that holds the status it deserves.

SATOMURA:
You're saying that each Japanese person should feel this way?

KUNIO NAKAGAWA:
Yeah. It's a horrible thing that two Japanese people were killed [in ISIL]. But the thing is, we're a nation that has purchased an immense amount of oil from those oil-producing countries and supported their economy to such a large extent that we seriously do

deserve a higher level of authority. We should be getting authority and respect.

SATOMURA:
You're saying that we should become a respected nation?

KUNIO NAKAGAWA:
It's very important to function properly as a nation. In other words, it's important to clearly say things that should be said.

SATOMURA:
Absolutely. The Happy Science Group, or the Happiness Realization Party, will work hard to turn Japan into that kind of nation.

"There will be a revolution of the times"

KUNIO NAKAGAWA:
People keep talking about the Yasukuni problem, but ultimately, the real issue is "scientific socialism" that comes from scientific materialism and Marxism-Leninism, right? And that basically describes what Japan has become in this postwar era, right? China won't have any problem swallowing Japan as a whole if it

has that kind of philosophy. So, Japan has to change its core way of thinking to prevent that from happening.

However, the gods of this nation are fairly strong. We won't submit that easily.

SATOMURA:
Right. The people still don't understand the will of these gods, right?

KUNIO NAKAGAWA:
No, they don't. Anyhow, we [the gods of Japan] are strong. There will be a revolution of the times.

SATOMURA:
Definitely. We'll keep working hard for that purpose, here on earth.

KUNIO NAKAGAWA:
Good, good.

SATOMURA:
[*To the other interviewers.*] Shall we stop here for today? OK, thank you very much for spending such a long time with us today and talking to us about so many different things.

KUNIO NAKAGAWA:
Sure thing. I want the people to really understand that there is something you should fear about more than death and that people can't fight if it isn't for love.

SATOMURA:
Thank you. We'll do our best to convey that.

KUNIO NAKAGAWA:
OK.

AYAORI & SATOMURA:
Thank you very much.

10

Praying that the Spiritual Messages from Colonel Nakagawa Will Influence Public Opinion

OKAWA:
All right. [*Claps once.*] He has an extremely pure state of mind.

SATOMURA:
Yes.

OKAWA:
He's quite the man. He fought a battle to death for over 70 days, which must've been a horrible experience. I'm sure he was a respectable person. That's my impression.

SATOMURA:
Yes.

OKAWA:
I guess the Japanese people must reflect back on post-war history. This is the responsibility of those who were born after the war.

• CLOSING COMMENTS •

SATOMURA:
Yes.

OKAWA:
I feel that the general trend started to change right around the release of the movie, *The Eternal Zero**. Both lines of thought will probably bump up against each other for some while longer. But the point is this: "People who fight to protect the country and to allow it to grow and prosper are respectable."

I would like to pray that sending out this spiritual message, before the emperor's visit to Palau, will have some kind of influence on public opinion.

SATOMURA:
We'll make efforts to ensure this message gets out to many people.

OKAWA:
OK. Thank you very much.

INTERVIEWERS:
Thank you very much.

---

* The Eternal Zero: a Japanese box-office hit movie, based on the novel of the same title, that was released in December 2013. It depicted the life and family love of a kamikaze Zero pilot during WWII.

Afterword

My opinion is that we're better off without war. In this meaning, I'm very glad that, even though we maintained one-country pacifism for 70 years since the end of the war, the Japanese people have enjoyed an era of peace and prosperity.

The flip side of this, however, has been that "the need for scientific proof" became prevalent and that the religious spirit and God's Justice were removed from education and ethics. This is very unfortunate.

It's also shameful that we have gone too far in our will to reflect on the war and have thus become subservient, lost the ability to discern good from evil and developed the national tendency to give convenient excuses in order to avoid facing the truth.

The Greater East Asia War was, in part, the will of the gods of Japan. It was true that Japan wished to liberate fellow Asians from colonial control of the Western superpowers. I would like to declare this and move toward building a new nation.

Ryuho Okawa
Master and CEO of Happy Science Group
March 3, 2015

About the Author

MASTER RYUHO OKAWA started receiving spiritual messages from Heaven in 1981. Holy beings appeared before him with impassioned messages of urgency, entreating him to deliver God's words to Earth. Within the same year, Master Okawa's deepest subconscious awakened and revealed his calling to become a spiritual leader who is inspiring the world with the power of God's Truths. Through these conversations with divine beings and through profound spiritual contemplation, Master Okawa developed the philosophy that would become the core of his teachings. His communications with Heaven deepened his understanding of God's designs and intentions—how He created our souls, this world, the other world, and the Laws that are the very fabric of the universe.

In 1986, Master Okawa founded Happy Science, a nondenominational universal religion, to share God's Truths and to help humankind overcome religious and cultural conflicts and usher in an era of peace on Earth. As part of the Happy Science movement, Master Okawa founded a political party, the Happiness Realization Party, as well as a private middle and high school, Happy Science Academy.

Lecture Broadcasted in Over 3,500 Places Around the World

Since he established Happy Science in 1986, Master Ryuho Okawa has given more than 2,300 lectures. This photo is from the Celebration of Lord's Descent Lecture Event held at Saitama Super Arena in Japan, on July 8, 2014. In the lecture titled, "The Grand Strategy for Prosperity," Master taught that we should not rely on a large government and, should an ambitious country appear, we must teach its people what the right way is. He also taught that it is important to build a future of peace in prosperity with every independent individual's efforts and perseverance. Over 17,000 people attended the main stadium and the event was also broadcasted live in over 3,500 places around the world.

Over 1,800 Books Published

Master Ryuho Okawa's books have been translated into 27 languages and the readership is growing around the world. In 2010, he received a Guinness World Record for publishing 52 books in a year and in 2013, he published 106 books within a year. As of the end of December 2014, the number of books published reached 1,800.

Among them there are also a lot of spiritual messages [see next page] from the spirits of historical greats and the guardian spirits of important figures living in the current world.

What is a Spiritual Message?

We are all spiritual beings living on this earth. The following is the mechanism behind Master Ryuho Okawa's spiritual messages.

1 You are a spirit

People are born into this world to gain wisdom through various experiences and return to the other world when their lives end. We are all spirits and repeat this cycle in order to refine our souls.

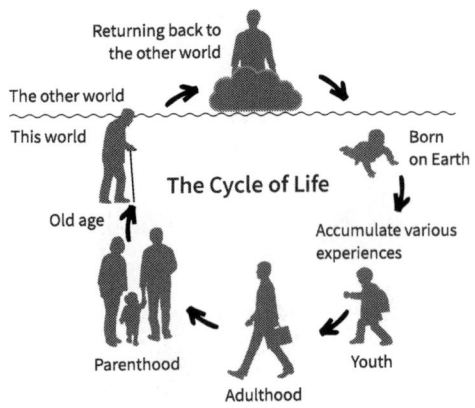

2 You have a guardian spirit

Guardian spirits are those who protect the people who are living on this earth. Each of us has a guardian spirit that watches over us and guides us from the other world. They were us in our past life, and are identical in how we think.

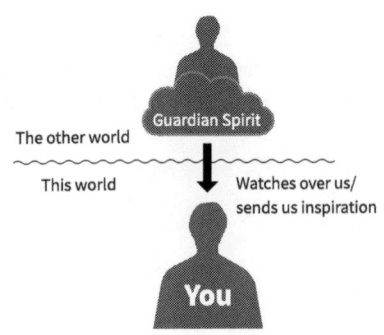

3 How spiritual messages work

Since guardian spirits think at the same subconscious level as the person living on earth, Master Okawa can summon the spirit and find out what the person on earth is actually thinking. If the person has already returned to the other world, the spirit can give messages to the people living on earth through Master Okawa.

1. The guardian spirit / spirit in the other world...
2. Goes inside Master Okawa in this world
3. Master Okawa speaks the words of the guardian spirit / spirit

The spiritual messages of more than 200 spirits have been recorded by Master Okawa since 2010, and the majority of these have been published. Spiritual messages from the guardian spirits of living politicians such as U.S. President Obama, Japanese Prime Minister Shinzo Abe and Chinese President Xi Jinping, as well as spiritual messages sent from the spirit world by Jesus Christ, Muhammad, Thomas Edison, Mother Teresa, Steve Jobs and Nelson Mandela are just a tiny pack of spiritual messages that were published so far.

Domestically, in Japan, these spiritual messages are being read by a wide range of politicians and mass media, and the high-level contents of these books are delivering an impact even more on politics, news and public opinion. In recent years, there have been spiritual messages recorded in English, and English translations are being done on the spiritual messages given in Japanese. These have been published overseas, one after another, and have started to shake the world.

For more about spiritual messages and a complete list of books in the Spiritual Interview Series, visit spiritualinterview.com

About Happy Science

In 1986, Master Ryuho Okawa founded Happy Science, a spiritual movement dedicated to bringing greater happiness to humankind by overcoming barriers of race, religion, and culture and by working toward the ideal of a world united in peace and harmony. Supported by followers who live in accordance with Master Okawa's words of enlightened wisdom, Happy Science has grown rapidly since its beginnings in Japan and now extends throughout the world. Today, it has twelve million members around the globe, with faith centers in New York, Los Angeles, San Francisco, Tokyo, London, Sydney, Sao Paulo, and Hong Kong, among many other major cities. Master Okawa speaks at Happy Science centers and travels around the world giving public lectures. Happy Science provides a variety of programs and services to support local communities. These programs include preschools, after-school educational programs for youths, and services for senior citizens and the disabled. Members also participate in social and charitable activities, which in the past have included providing relief aid to earthquake victims in China, New Zealand, and Turkey, and to flood victims in Thailand as well as building schools in Sri Lanka.

Programs and Events

Happy Science faith centers offer regular events, programs, and seminars. Join our meditation sessions, video lectures, study groups, seminars, and book events. Our programs will help you:
- Deepen your understanding of the purpose and meaning of life
- Improve your relationships as you learn how to love unconditionally
- Learn how to calm your mind even on stressful days through the practice of contemplation and meditation
- Learn how to overcome life's challenges
  ...and much more.

International Seminars

Each year, friends from all over the world join our international seminars, held at our faith centers in Japan. Different programs are offered each year and cover a wide variety of topics, including improving relationships, practicing the Eightfold Path to enlightenment, and loving yourself, to name just a few.

Happy Science Monthly

Read Master Okawa's latest lectures in our monthly booklet, Happy Science Monthly. You'll also find stories of members' life-changing experiences, news from Happy Science members around the world, in-depth information about Happy Science movies, book reviews, and much more. Happy Science Monthly is available in English, Portuguese, Chinese, and other languages. Back issues are available upon request. Subscribe by contacting the Happy Science location nearest you.

Contact Information

Happy Science is a worldwide organization with faith centers around the globe. For a comprehensive list of centers, visit the worldwide directory at http://www.happy-science.org or www.happyscience-na.org.

The following are some of the many Happy Science locations:

United States and Canada

New York
79 Franklin Street, New York, NY 10013, U.S.A.
TEL 1-212-343-7972
FAX 1-212-343-7973
Email: ny@happy-science.org
Website: www.happyscience-ny.org

Los Angeles
1590 E. Del Mar Blvd., Pasadena, CA 91106, U.S.A.
Phone: 1-626-395-7775
Fax: 1-626-395-7776
Email: la@happy-science.org
Website: www.happyscience-la.org

San Diego
Email: sandiego@happy-science.org

San Francisco
525 Clinton Street, Redwood City, CA 94062, U.S.A.
Phone/Fax: 1-650-363-2777
Email: sf@happy-science.org
Website: www.happyscience-sf.org

Atlanta
1874 Piedmont Ave., NE Suite 360-C Atlanta, GA 30324, U.S.A.
Phone/Fax: 1-404-892-7770
Email: atlanta@happy-science.org
Website: www.atlanta.happyscience-na.org

Florida
12208 N 56th Street
Temple Terrace, FL 33617
Phone:1-813-914-7771
Fax: 1-813-914-7710
Email: florida@happy-science.org
Website: www.happyscience-fl.org

New Jersey
725 River Road, Suite 200
Edgewater, NJ 07025
Phone: 1-201-313-0127
Fax: 1-201-313-0120
Email: nj@happy-science.org
Website: www.happyscience-nj.org

Hawaii (Oahu)
1221 Kapiolani Blvd., Suite 920
Honolulu, HI 96814, U.S.A.
Phone: 1-808-591-9772
Fax: 1-808-591-9776
Email: hi@happy-science.org
Website: www.happyscience-hi.org

Hawaii (Kauai)
4504 Kukui Street
Dragon Building Suite 21
Kapaa, HI 96746
Phone: 1-808-822-7007
Fax: 1-808-822-6007
Email: kauai-hi@happy-science.org
Website: www.happyscience-kauai.org

Toronto
323 College Street.,
Toronto On. Canada M5T 1S2
Phone/Fax: 1-416-901-3747
Email: toronto@happy-science.org
Website: www.happy-science.ca

Vancouver
#212-2609 East 49th Avenue,
Vancouver, V5S 1J9, Canada
Phone: 1-604-437-7735
Fax: 1-604-437-7764
Email: vancouver@happy-science.org
Website: www.happy-science.ca

International

Tokyo
1-6-7 Togoshi, Shinagawa,
Tokyo, 142-0041 Japan
Phone: 81-3-6384-5770
Fax: 81-3-6384-5776
Email: tokyo@happy-science.org
Website: www.happy-science.org

London
3 Margaret Street,
London, W1W 8RE, United Kingdom
Phone: 44-20-7323-9255
Fax: 44-20-7323-9344
Email: eu@happy-science.org
Website: www.happyscience-uk.org

Seoul
162-17 Sadang3-dong,
Dongjak-gu, Seoul, South Korea
Phone: 82-2-3478-8777
Fax: 82-2-3478-9777
Email: korea@happy-science.org
Website: www.happyscience-korea.org

Taipei
No.89, Lane 155,
Dunhua N. Road.,
Songshan District,
Taipei City 105, Taiwan
Phone: 886-2-2719-9377
Fax: 886-2-2719-5570
Email: taiwan@happy-science.org
Website: www.happyscience-tw.org

Sydney
516 Pacific Highway, Lane Cove
North, NSW 2066, Australia
Phone: 61-2-9411-2877
Fax: 61-2-9411-2822
Email: sydney@happy-science.org
Website: www.happyscience.org.au

Brazil Headquarters
R. Domingos de Morais 1154,
Vila Mariana, Sao Paulo, SP-CEP
04009-002, Brazil
Phone: 55-11-5088-3800
Fax: 55-11-5088-3806
Email: sp@happy-science.org
Website: www.happyscience-br.org

Uganda
Plot 877 Rubaga Road, Kampala,
P.O. Box 34130, Kampala,
Uganda
Phone: 256-79-3238-002
Email: uganda@happy-science.org
Website: www.happyscience-uganda.org

Nepal
Kathmandu Metropolitan City,
Ring Road, Sitapaila,
Kimdol, Ward No.15,
Harati Marg, Kathmandu, Nepal
TEL 977-1-4272931
Email: nepal@happy-science.org

About the Happiness Realization Party

The Happiness Realization Party (HRP) was founded in May 2009 by Master Ryuho Okawa as part of the Happy Science Group to offer concrete and proactive solutions to the current issues such as military threats from North Korea and China and the long-term economic recession. HRP aims to implement drastic reforms of the Japanese government, thereby bringing peace and prosperity to Japan. To accomplish this, HRP proposes two key policies:

1) Strengthening the national security and the Japan-US alliance which plays a vital role in the stability of Asia.
2) Improving the Japanese economy by implementing drastic tax cuts, taking monetary easing measures and creating new major industries.

HRP advocates that Japan should offer a model of a religious nation that allows diverse values and beliefs to coexist, and that contributes to global peace.

For more information, please visit www.hr-party.jp

Happy Science University
* This is an unaccredited institution of higher education.

The Founding Spirit and the Goal of Education
Based on the founding philosophy of the university, "Pursuit of happiness and the creation of a new civilization," education, research and studies will be provided to help students acquire deep understanding grounded in religious belief and advanced expertise with the objectives of producing "great talents of virtue" who can contribute in a broad-ranging way to serve Japan and the international society.

Overview of Faculties and Departments
- Faculty of Human Happiness, Department of Human Happiness

Students in this faculty will pursue liberal arts from various perspectives with a multidisciplinary approach, explore and envision an idea state of human beings and society.

- Faculty of Successful Management, Department of Successful management

This faculty aims to realize successful management that helps organizational entities of all kinds to create value and wealth for society and to contribute to the happiness and the development of management and employees as well as society as a whole.

- Faculty of Future Industry, Department of Industrial Technology

This faculty aims to nurture engineers who can resolve various issues facing modern civilization from a technological standpoint and contribute to the creation of new industries of the future.

Happy Science Academy
Junior and Senior High School

Happy Science Academy Junior and Senior High School is a boarding school founded with the goal of educating the future leaders of the world who can have a big vision, persevere, and take on new challenges. Currently, there are two campuses in Japan; the Nasu Main Campus in Tochigi Prefecture, founded in 2010, and the Kansai Campus in Shiga Prefecture, founded in 2013.

Other Activities

Happy Science does other various activities to provide support for those in need.

Success NO.1
Buddha's Truth Afterschool Academy

Happy Science has over 180 classrooms throughout Japan and in several cities around the world that focuses on afterschool education for children. The education focuses on faith and morals in addition to supporting children's school studies.

Angel Plan V

For children under the age of kindergarten, Happy Science holds classes for nurturing healthy, positive, and creative boys and girls.

The Golden Age Scholarship

This scholarship is granted to students who can contribute greatly and bring a hopeful future to the world.

Never Mind School for Truancy

At 'Never Mind,' we support students who find it very challenging to attend schools. We also nurture their self-help spirit and power to rebound against obstacles in life based on Master Okawa's teachings and faith.

"You Are an Angel!" project

Happy Science has a volunteer network that encourages and supports children with disabilities as well as their parents and guardians.

The Helen Society

Happy Science supports visually and hearing impaired people to study the Truth. By learning the Truth, they are able to study about this world and the spirit world, make themselves better, overcome their obstacles, and be able to live a bright life.

Future Stars Training Department

The Future Star's Training Department was founded within the Happy Science Media Division with the goal of nurturing talented individuals to become successful in the performing arts and entertainment industry.

New Star Production Co., Ltd.

We also have a company to nurture actors and actresses, artists, and vocalists. It is also involved in film production.

Art and Culture Festival

The Art and Culture Festival is held once a year with the hope of promoting religious art. Winners are given opportunities to further promote their art and pursue their passion.

About IRH Press

IRH Press Co., Ltd, based in Tokyo, was founded in 1987 as a publishing division of Happy Science. IRH Press publishes religious and spiritual books, journals, magazines and also operates broadcast and film production enterprises. For more information, visit OkawaBooks.com.

Other Books by Ryuho Okawa

THE LAWS OF WISDOM
Shine Your Diamond Within

This book guides you along the path on how to acquire wisdom, so that you can break through any wall you are facing or will confront in your life or in your business. By reading this book, you will be able to avoid getting lost in the flood of information and go beyond the level of just amassing knowledge. You will be able to come up with many great ideas, make effective planning and strategy and develop your leadership while receiving good inspiration.

THE LAWS OF PERSEVERANCE
Reversing Your Common Sense

"No matter how much you suffer, the Truth will gradually shine forth as you continue to endure hardships. Therefore, simply strengthen your mind and keep making constant efforts in times of endurance, however ordinary they may be."

–From Postscript

THE LAWS OF INVINCIBLE LEADERSHIP
How To Keep On Succeeding

"I wish strongly for all people to attain this true happiness that will persist through the afterlife. With this profound desire, I encourage everyone to aspire to be an invincible winner. I hope that this book will give courage and wisdom to millions of readers today and countless people in the generations to come."

–From Preface

For a complete list of books, visit okawabooks.com

THE LAWS OF THE SUN
ONE SOURCE, ONE PLANET, ONE PEOPLE

IMAGINE IF YOU COULD ASK GOD why He created this world and what spiritual laws He used to shape us—and everything around us. If we could understand His designs and intentions, we could discover what our goals in life should be and whether our actions move us closer to those goals or farther away.

THE GOLDEN LAWS
HISTORY THROUGH THE EYES OF THE ETERNAL BUDDHA

The Golden Laws reveals how Buddha's Plan has been unfolding on earth, and outlines five thousand years of the secret history of humankind. Once we understand the true course of history, we cannot help but become aware of the significance of our spiritual mission in the present age.

THE NINE DIMENSIONS
UNVEILING THE LAWS OF ETERNITY

This book is a window into the mind of our loving God, who encourages us to grow into greater angels. It reveals His deepest intentions, answering the timely question of why He conceived such a colorful medley of religions, philosophies, sciences, arts, and other forms of expression.

For a complete list of books, visit okawabooks.com

Spiritual Interview Series

THE TRUTH OF THE PACIFIC WAR
SOULFUL MESSAGES FROM HIDEKI TOJO, JAPAN'S WARTIME LEADER
INCLUDING A SPIRITUAL INTERVIEW WITH GENERAL DOUGLAS MACARTHUR

The material provided is a testimony by General Hideki Tojo, who was Japan's most significant figure in the Pacific War. Furthermore, we have also recorded a testimony by Supreme Commander of the Allied Powers Douglas MacArthur in order to ensure a fair argument.

WHAT REALLY HAPPENED IN NANKING?
A SPIRITUAL TESTIMONY OF THE HONORABLE JAPANESE COMMANDER IWANE MATSUI

"This book is a spiritual interview with General Iwane Matsui, who was the commanding officer during the Battle of Nanking. Will we give in to the extortion by the mere ex-prostitutes, toward the Japanese government, in their 90s who are claiming that they were military comfort women? Will we give Xi Jinping a reason for his imperialist invasion policy of the 21st century? This book will likely put a firm end to those debates." -From Preface

THE SECRET BEHIND "THE RAPE OF NANKING"
A SPIRITUAL CONFESSION BY IRIS CHANG

There is a phrase, "History is written by the victors." If a fabricated history had spread throughout the world, it must be corrected in an objective and impartial manner. Iris Chang confessed the truth regarding the content of her book, *The Rape of Nanking*, and its background, just 10 years after her death, in a form of a spiritual message.

For a complete list of books, visit okawabooks.com

JAPAN! REGAIN YOUR SAMURAI SPIRIT

A MESSAGE FROM THE GUARDIAN SPIRIT OF LEE TENG-HUI, FORMER PRESIDENT OF THE REPUBLIC OF CHINA

This book is the record of interviews conducted on Former President of Taiwan Lee Teng-hui's guardian spirit in February 2014. His true thoughts, as well as the truth on modern East-Asian history, were revealed in these interviews.

THE TRUTH OF NANKING AND COMFORT WOMEN ISSUES

A SPIRITUAL READING INTO WORLD WAR II BY EDGAR CAYCE

This book is a spiritual guidebook that will answer all your questions about the spiritual world, with illustrations and diagrams explaining about your guardian spirit and the secrets of God and Buddha. By reading this book, you will be able to understand the true meaning of life and find happiness in everyday life.

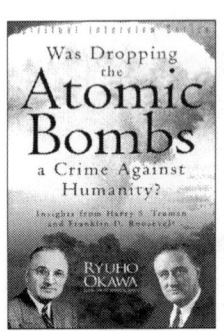

WAS DROPPING THE ATOMIC BOMBS A CRIME AGAINST HUMANITY?

INSIGHTS FROM HARRY S. TRUMAN AND FRANKLIN D. ROOSEVELT

Was there any true justification for the atomic bombing of Hiroshima and Nagasaki? Could anything justify the use of nuclear weapons on civilians? This book reveals valuable information that will help the world gain a truthful understanding of world history.

For a complete list of books, visit okawabooks.com

IRH Movies

Master Okawa is the creator and executive producer of nine films. These movies have received various awards and recognition around the world.

Movie Titles :
- The Terrifying Revelations of Nostradamus (1994)
- Love Blows Like the Wind (1997)
- The Laws of the Sun (2000)
- The Golden Laws (2003)
- The Laws of Eternity (2006)
- The Rebirth of Buddha (2009)
- The Final Judgement (2012)
- The Mystical Laws (2012)

The Mystical Laws

The winner of
"2013 Remi Special Jury Award"
for Theatrical Feature Productions in
WorldFest Houston International Film Festival

Other Awards:
- "Palm Beach International Film Festival" Nominated for Best Feature Official Selection
- "Asian Film Festival of Dallas" Official selection
- "Proctors 4th Annual Animation Festival" Official Selection
- "Buddhist Film Festival Europe" Official Selection
- "Japan Film Fest Hamburg" Official Selection
- "Monstra,the Lisbon Animated Film Festival" Official Selection

Now available on
Video On Demand, visit
mystical-laws.com

Coming soon **in Fall 2015**
The Laws of the Universe
- Part 0

For more information, visit **hspicturesstudio.com**

Made in the USA
Lexington, KY
28 June 2015